INTELLIGENT DOCUMENT PROCESSING (IDP)

A Comprehensive Guide to Streamlining Document Management

Rick Spair

Introduction

The world of document management is evolving rapidly, and organizations are increasingly turning to Intelligent Document Processing (IDP) to streamline their document management processes. This comprehensive guide serves as a valuable resource for individuals and organizations embarking on their IDP journey. It offers a step-by-step approach, practical tips, and best practices to help readers successfully implement IDP and achieve significant improvements in efficiency, accuracy, and cost savings.

In today's digital age, the volume and complexity of documents continue to grow exponentially, posing significant challenges for organizations across industries. Traditional manual document management processes are time-consuming, error-prone, and resource-intensive, leading to inefficiencies and missed opportunities. However, the advent of Intelligent Document Processing (IDP) presents a game-changing solution.

Intelligent Document Processing combines the power of artificial intelligence, machine learning, and automation technologies to extract and process data from unstructured documents swiftly and accurately. By automating manual tasks, organizations can enhance productivity, improve data accuracy, and optimize their document management workflows. This guide serves as a roadmap for readers looking to harness the potential of IDP and transform their document management practices.

The chapters of this guide take readers on a comprehensive journey through the world of IDP. It begins with an introduction to document management and the concept of Intelligent Document Processing. Readers will gain a clear understanding of the benefits and importance of implementing IDP in their organizations.

The guide then delves into the key aspects of implementing IDP. It covers topics such as assessing document management needs, identifying document types and formats, analyzing document volume and complexity, and evaluating existing document management processes. These chapters provide practical insights, tips, and strategies to help readers assess their current state and identify areas for improvement.

As the journey progresses, the guide dives into creating an IDP strategy, including setting clear goals and objectives, selecting the right IDP solution, and defining key performance indicators (KPIs). It emphasizes the importance of customization and adaptation to align with specific organizational needs and goals.

The guide further explores preparing documents for IDP, including standardizing formats and layouts, optimizing image quality and resolution, and implementing document classification and indexing. It provides detailed guidance on leveraging intelligent capture technologies, extracting data from structured and unstructured documents, and validating and verifying extracted data.

The chapters also cover crucial aspects such as integrating IDP with existing systems, monitoring and measuring IDP performance, change management, and user adoption. They address data security and compliance requirements, as well as provide real-world case studies and success stories to inspire and educate readers.

Throughout the guide, readers will find tips, recommendations, and best practices from industry leaders who have successfully implemented IDP. These insights serve as valuable lessons learned and provide practical guidance for readers as they embark on their IDP journey.

In conclusion, this comprehensive guide equips readers with the knowledge and tools needed to implement Intelligent Document Processing successfully. By following the chapters, tips, recommendations, and strategies outlined in this guide, organizations can streamline their document management processes, achieve significant improvements in efficiency and accuracy, and drive tangible business outcomes. The IDP journey begins here, offering endless possibilities for optimizing document management in the digital era.

CONTENTS

Chapter 22: D & C

CHAPTER 1: INTRODUCTION TO DOCUMENT MANAGEMENT AND INTELLIGENT DOCUMENT PROCESSING

Overview: In today's digital age, businesses and organizations generate and handle a vast amount of documents, both in physical and digital formats. Effectively managing these documents is crucial for maintaining efficiency, productivity, and compliance. This chapter serves as an introduction to document management and explores the concept of Intelligent Document Processing (IDP), a transformative technology that leverages artificial intelligence (AI) and automation to streamline document-centric processes.

1.1 Definition and Importance of Document Management: This section provides a clear definition of document management, which encompasses the creation, storage, retrieval, and disposal of documents throughout their lifecycle. It highlights the significance of efficient document management in terms of reducing manual errors, enhancing collaboration, ensuring regulatory compliance, and improving overall productivity.

1.2 Introduction to Intelligent Document Processing (IDP): Here, the focus shifts to IDP, an advanced technology that combines machine learning, natural language processing, and optical character recognition (OCR) to automate document-related tasks. IDP enables organizations to extract valuable data from documents, classify them, and automate workflows, leading to improved accuracy, faster processing times, and reduced operational costs.

1.3 Benefits of Implementing IDP: This section outlines the numerous advantages that organizations can derive from implementing IDP. Key benefits include:

- Time and Cost Savings: IDP automates manual tasks, reducing the time and effort required for document processing and data extraction.

- Improved Accuracy: Machine learning algorithms enhance accuracy, minimizing errors and the need for manual intervention.
- Enhanced Compliance: IDP ensures compliance with regulations by capturing and managing documents according to specific guidelines.
- Increased Productivity: Automation and streamlined workflows result in improved productivity and efficiency.
- Better Decision-Making: Access to extracted data enables data-driven decision-making and actionable insights.

1.4 Key Challenges in Document Management: To set realistic expectations, this section highlights some common challenges that organizations may face when managing documents. These challenges include:

- High document volumes and diverse formats
- Manual data entry and repetitive tasks
- Data security and privacy concerns
- Document retrieval and version control issues
- Compliance with industry regulations

1.5 The IDP Journey: The final part of this chapter introduces the concept of the IDP journey, emphasizing that successful implementation of IDP requires a strategic approach. It emphasizes the need to assess current document management practices, set goals, select appropriate IDP solutions, and establish performance metrics for tracking progress. The IDP journey is an ongoing process of optimization and continuous improvement.

By understanding the fundamentals of document management and the transformative potential of IDP, organizations can lay the foundation for a successful IDP implementation and embark on the journey to optimize their document-centric processes.

Definition and Importance of Document Management

Document management refers to the systematic process of creating, organizing, storing, retrieving, and disposing of documents throughout their lifecycle. It involves the management of both physical and digital documents in a way that ensures efficient access, accurate information retrieval, and regulatory compliance. Document management encompasses various activities, including document creation, version control, indexing, categorization, storage, security, collaboration, and document disposal.

In today's fast-paced business environment, effective document management is crucial for organizations of all sizes and industries. Here are some key reasons why document management is important:

1. Organization and Efficiency: Document management enables organizations to maintain a structured and organized approach to handling documents. It provides a centralized repository where documents can be stored, categorized, and accessed easily. With efficient document management, employees can quickly locate the information they need, reducing time wasted searching for documents and improving overall productivity.
2. Reduced Errors and Improved Accuracy: Manual document handling processes are prone to errors, such as misplacing or losing important documents, entering incorrect data, or using outdated versions. Document management systems streamline these processes, minimizing the risk of errors and ensuring that accurate and up-to-date information is readily available. This improves the quality of work and reduces the chances of making costly mistakes.
3. Enhanced Collaboration and Communication: Document management facilitates seamless collaboration among team members, departments, and even external stakeholders. With a centralized document repository, multiple users can access, edit, and share documents simultaneously. This fosters effective communication, encourages knowledge sharing, and promotes collaborative work practices, leading to increased productivity and improved decision-making.

4. Regulatory Compliance: Organizations across various industries must comply with regulations governing document retention, data security, and privacy. Document management systems help meet these requirements by implementing appropriate security measures, tracking document access and modifications, and providing audit trails. Compliance with regulations not only reduces legal risks but also builds trust with customers and stakeholders.
5. Cost Savings and Space Optimization: Traditional paper-based document management systems are not only time-consuming but also expensive. Storing, organizing, and retrieving physical documents can be labor-intensive and resource-draining. Adopting digital document management solutions reduces paper usage, lowers printing and storage costs, and optimizes office space. Furthermore, digital documents are easily accessible and can be shared instantly, eliminating the need for physical document transportation and distribution.
6. Disaster Recovery and Business Continuity: Natural disasters, accidents, or technical failures can pose significant risks to document integrity and accessibility. Document management systems provide backup and disaster recovery capabilities, ensuring that documents are safely stored and can be recovered in the event of a disruption. This helps organizations maintain business continuity and minimize potential losses caused by document loss or damage.
7. Improved Customer Service: Efficient document management directly impacts customer service by enabling faster response times, accurate information retrieval, and streamlined processes. Quick access to customer-related documents allows employees to provide timely and accurate support, resulting in improved customer satisfaction and loyalty.

In summary, document management plays a vital role in modern organizations. By implementing effective document management strategies and leveraging technology solutions, businesses can enhance productivity, reduce errors, ensure regulatory compliance, optimize costs, and improve overall operational efficiency. Whether it is streamlining internal workflows, complying with industry regulations, or providing exceptional customer service, document management is an indispensable tool for organizations seeking to stay competitive in today's digital landscape.

Introduction to Intelligent Document Processing (IDP)

In today's digital era, organizations face the challenge of managing an ever-increasing volume of documents. Intelligent Document Processing (IDP) emerges as a transformative technology that leverages artificial intelligence (AI) and automation to revolutionize document-centric processes. This chapter provides an introduction to IDP, exploring its definition, core components, and the significant benefits it offers to organizations.

Definition of Intelligent Document Processing (IDP): Intelligent Document Processing (IDP) refers to the use of AI technologies, including machine learning, natural language processing (NLP), and optical character recognition (OCR), to automate and streamline document-centric tasks. IDP systems are designed to intelligently capture, classify, extract, validate, and manage data from various types of documents, both structured and unstructured. By mimicking human intelligence, IDP solutions enable organizations to extract valuable information from documents accurately and efficiently, leading to improved operational efficiency, enhanced data accuracy, and faster decision-making.

Core Components of IDP: IDP encompasses several core components that work together to automate document processing tasks:

1. Optical Character Recognition (OCR): OCR technology converts printed or handwritten text into machine-readable formats. It enables IDP systems to extract text from scanned or digital documents, making it searchable and editable.
2. Machine Learning (ML): Machine learning algorithms enable IDP systems to learn from data patterns and make accurate predictions or decisions. ML models can be trained to classify

documents, extract relevant data, and continuously improve performance over time.

3. Natural Language Processing (NLP): NLP enables IDP systems to understand and interpret human language. It helps extract meaningful information from unstructured documents, such as contracts, emails, or invoices, by analyzing the text's syntax, semantics, and sentiment.
4. Data Extraction and Validation: IDP solutions extract relevant data fields from documents, such as customer names, addresses, invoice numbers, or purchase details. These extracted data can be validated against predefined rules or compared with existing databases to ensure accuracy and completeness.
5. Document Classification: IDP systems employ classification algorithms to categorize documents based on their content, format, or purpose. This enables automated routing, sorting, and archiving of documents, improving overall document management efficiency.

Benefits of IDP: Implementing IDP offers organizations a wide range of benefits, including:

1. Time and Cost Savings: IDP eliminates manual data entry and document processing, reducing time-consuming tasks and associated labor costs. Automated document handling accelerates processing times, enabling organizations to complete tasks faster and improve overall productivity.
2. Enhanced Accuracy: By leveraging AI technologies, IDP significantly reduces human errors that may occur during manual data entry or document processing. ML models continuously learn from data patterns, resulting in improved accuracy over time.
3. Improved Efficiency: IDP streamlines document-centric workflows, allowing organizations to automate repetitive tasks and allocate resources to higher-value activities. This improves operational efficiency and enables employees to focus on more strategic and complex tasks.

4. Scalability and Flexibility: IDP solutions are scalable, allowing organizations to handle large volumes of documents efficiently. As businesses grow, IDP systems can adapt to changing document processing requirements without the need for extensive manual intervention.
5. Data-Driven Decision-Making: IDP enables organizations to extract valuable insights from document data. By leveraging accurate and timely information, decision-makers can make data-driven decisions, improve strategic planning, and gain a competitive advantage.
6. Compliance and Auditability: IDP systems provide enhanced compliance capabilities by capturing, storing, and managing documents in accordance with regulatory requirements. They also offer audit trails, ensuring transparency and accountability in document handling processes.
7. Improved Customer Experience: IDP enables organizations to respond faster to customer queries, process transactions quickly, and provide accurate information. This leads to improved customer satisfaction, loyalty, and a better overall customer experience.

Conclusion: Intelligent Document Processing (IDP) is a game-changer for organizations looking to streamline document-centric processes. By leveraging AI technologies, IDP solutions offer numerous benefits, including time and cost savings, enhanced accuracy, improved efficiency, and data-driven decision-making. Implementing IDP enables organizations to optimize document management, achieve operational excellence, and gain a competitive edge in today's fast-paced business landscape.

Benefits of Implementing Intelligent Document Processing (IDP)

Implementing Intelligent Document Processing (IDP) offers numerous benefits to organizations across various industries. By leveraging artificial intelligence (AI) and automation technologies, IDP revolutionizes document-centric processes, enabling organizations to streamline operations, improve efficiency, and unlock valuable insights from their documents. In this chapter, we explore the key benefits of implementing IDP.

1. Time and Cost Savings: IDP eliminates manual and time-consuming document processing tasks, such as data entry and manual data extraction. By automating these processes, organizations can significantly reduce the time required to handle documents. This frees up valuable employee time, allowing them to focus on more strategic and high-value tasks. Moreover, automating document processing with IDP reduces the need for manual labor, leading to cost savings in terms of reduced staffing requirements and increased operational efficiency.
2. Enhanced Accuracy: Manual document processing is prone to human errors, such as typos, incorrect data entry, or misinterpretation of information. IDP leverages AI technologies like machine learning and natural language processing to improve accuracy. Machine learning algorithms can be trained on a large dataset to recognize patterns, extract data accurately, and validate information against predefined rules. As IDP systems learn and adapt over time, they continually improve accuracy, resulting in more reliable data extraction and reduced error rates.
3. Improved Efficiency and Productivity: IDP automates repetitive and mundane document processing tasks, eliminating the need for manual intervention. This automation significantly increases operational efficiency by reducing processing times, improving throughput, and eliminating bottlenecks in document workflows. Employees can focus on value-added activities that require critical thinking and expertise, enhancing overall productivity. By streamlining document-centric processes, IDP enables organizations to handle higher document volumes without the need for additional resources.
4. Enhanced Data Accessibility and Searchability: IDP solutions convert documents into searchable and indexed formats, enabling quick and easy access to information. With IDP, users

can search for specific keywords, phrases, or data elements within documents, eliminating the need for time-consuming manual searches. This enhances data accessibility and speeds up information retrieval, enabling employees to find the information they need faster. By improving data accessibility, IDP also facilitates better collaboration among teams, departments, and stakeholders.

5. Better Decision-Making: IDP extracts valuable insights and data from documents, empowering organizations to make data-driven decisions. By automatically extracting and validating data, organizations can analyze trends, patterns, and anomalies within their document repository. This information provides valuable insights that can be used to identify opportunities, mitigate risks, improve operational efficiency, and make informed strategic decisions. With access to accurate and timely data, organizations can respond faster to market changes and gain a competitive advantage.
6. Regulatory Compliance: Organizations across various industries must comply with industry-specific regulations and standards regarding document management, data privacy, and security. IDP helps ensure compliance by capturing and managing documents according to regulatory requirements. IDP systems provide features such as audit trails, version control, and data encryption, enhancing document security and regulatory compliance. By automating compliance processes, organizations reduce the risk of errors and penalties associated with non-compliance.
7. Scalability and Adaptability: IDP solutions are scalable, allowing organizations to handle increasing document volumes efficiently. As businesses grow and document volumes expand, IDP systems can adapt and accommodate the increased workload without sacrificing performance. This scalability ensures that organizations can maintain operational efficiency even as document volumes continue to increase. Additionally, IDP solutions are adaptable to various document types and

formats, making them suitable for different industries and document-intensive workflows.

8. Improved Customer Experience: IDP enables organizations to provide a better customer experience by reducing response times, improving data accuracy, and streamlining customer-facing processes. With IDP, organizations can automate document-intensive processes such as

CHAPTER 2: ASSESSING YOUR DOCUMENT MANAGEMENT NEEDS

Overview: Before embarking on any document management initiative, it is essential to assess your organization's specific document management needs and requirements. This chapter focuses on guiding you through the process of assessing your document management needs effectively. By understanding your current document landscape, challenges, and goals, you can lay a solid foundation for developing an efficient and tailored document management strategy.

2.1 Understanding Document Types and Formats: This section emphasizes the importance of identifying and categorizing the different types and formats of documents used within your organization. It provides guidance on identifying physical documents, digital files, email communications, and other document sources. By understanding the diversity of document types, you can determine the necessary strategies and technologies required for managing each type effectively.

2.2 Determining Document Volume and Complexity: Assessing the volume and complexity of your document landscape is crucial in developing a scalable and efficient document management solution. This section guides you through analyzing the volume of documents generated, received, and processed within your organization on a daily, monthly, and yearly basis. It also explores the complexity of your documents, considering factors such as document structures, variations, and data extraction requirements.

2.3 Analyzing Existing Document Management Processes: This section focuses on evaluating your current document management processes. It involves assessing the efficiency, accuracy, and reliability of existing document workflows, from document creation to storage and retrieval. By identifying pain points, bottlenecks, and areas for improvement, you can lay the groundwork for enhancing document management processes.

2.4 Identifying Document Management Challenges: Understanding the challenges and pain points associated with your document management processes is crucial for finding suitable solutions. This section explores common challenges, such as manual data entry, document retrieval delays, compliance issues, version control problems, and security concerns. By identifying and documenting these challenges, you can prioritize solutions that address specific pain points and maximize the benefits of a document management system.

2.5 Defining Document Management Goals and Objectives: This section focuses on setting clear goals and objectives for your document management initiative. It helps you define what you aim to achieve through effective document management, such as improved efficiency, reduced costs, enhanced compliance, streamlined workflows, or better collaboration. By setting specific and measurable goals, you can track progress and ensure that your document management strategy aligns with your organization's broader objectives.

2.6 Assessing Technology Requirements: In this section, you will evaluate the technology requirements necessary to meet your document management needs. This includes considering the document management software, systems, and tools that align with your goals and requirements. It involves evaluating features such as document capture, storage, indexing, retrieval, security, and collaboration capabilities. By assessing technology requirements, you can identify suitable solutions that fit your organization's needs and budget.

2.7 Stakeholder Engagement and Collaboration: This section emphasizes the importance of involving key stakeholders in the assessment process. It guides you on engaging with various departments, teams, and individuals who are involved in document management. By understanding their perspectives, challenges, and requirements, you can ensure that your document management strategy is comprehensive and addresses the needs of all stakeholders.

2.8 Document Management Roadmap: The chapter concludes by emphasizing the importance of developing a document management roadmap. This involves synthesizing the findings from the assessment process and creating a plan that outlines the steps, timeline, and resources required for implementing your document management strategy. A well-defined roadmap provides a clear path for achieving your document management goals and ensures a smooth and successful implementation.

By effectively assessing your document management needs, challenges, and goals, you can lay the foundation for developing a tailored and efficient document management strategy. This assessment phase sets the stage for the subsequent chapters, where you will delve into selecting the right document management solutions, designing workflows, and implementing best practices for a successful document management journey.

Identifying Document Types and Formats

In the world of document management, understanding the various types and formats of documents is essential for developing an effective document management strategy. Different document types and formats have unique characteristics, requirements, and challenges associated with their management. This chapter focuses on guiding you through the process of identifying document types and formats within your organization. By gaining a comprehensive understanding of your document landscape, you can implement targeted strategies and technologies to manage each type effectively.

1. Physical Documents: Physical documents are tangible, paper-based records that exist in the form of letters, contracts, invoices, receipts, reports, and other printed materials. These documents often originate from external sources or are generated internally and require physical storage and handling. Identifying the types of physical documents in your organization is crucial for determining appropriate storage solutions, archival processes, and strategies for digitization and integration with digital workflows.
2. Digital Documents: Digital documents are electronic files created, stored, and accessed using various applications and file formats. These include word processing documents (e.g., Microsoft Word, Google Docs), spreadsheets (e.g., Microsoft Excel, Google Sheets), presentations (e.g., Microsoft PowerPoint, Google Slides), PDFs, images, and multimedia files. Digital documents can be created internally or received from external sources. Understanding the range of digital document formats used within your organization is essential for implementing compatible document management solutions and ensuring seamless access and retrieval.
3. Email Communications: Emails are a significant source of business-related documents, encompassing messages, attachments, and threaded conversations. Email

communications often contain critical information such as contracts, agreements, project updates, and client correspondence. Identifying and managing email communications effectively is essential for ensuring compliance, streamlining workflows, and centralizing important information within your document management system.

4. Web Content: Web content refers to documents and information found on websites, intranets, portals, and other online platforms. This includes web pages, blogs, articles, multimedia content, and downloadable files. With the increasing reliance on online sources for information sharing and collaboration, identifying and managing web content within your document management strategy becomes crucial. Techniques such as web scraping and content extraction may be required to capture and organize relevant web-based information.
5. Structured Documents: Structured documents are those that have a well-defined format and follow a specific schema or template. Examples include forms, surveys, questionnaires, and standardized reports. These documents often contain predefined fields, checkboxes, or data capture areas. Identifying structured documents is important for implementing automated data extraction and validation techniques, ensuring accurate and efficient processing of information.
6. Unstructured Documents: Unstructured documents lack a predefined format or consistent structure. They include narrative reports, memos, contracts, research papers, and other documents with varying layouts and content structures. Unstructured documents pose unique challenges for document management due to their complexity and the need for sophisticated techniques such as natural language processing (NLP) to extract relevant data. Identifying unstructured documents helps determine the appropriate methods and technologies for capturing and processing information effectively.
7. Specialized Document Types: Certain industries or organizations may have specialized document types specific to their operations. For example, in the healthcare sector, medical

records, prescriptions, and lab reports are critical document types. Legal firms deal with contracts, court filings, and legal correspondence. Identifying specialized document types relevant to your industry or organization helps tailor document management solutions to address specific compliance requirements, data extraction needs, and workflow optimizations.

8. Hybrid Documents: Hybrid documents are a combination of physical and digital elements. These documents may contain both printed and electronically captured data, such as handwritten notes on printed documents or annotations on digital files. Identifying hybrid documents is essential for understanding the unique challenges associated with their management, including digitization, data extraction, and preserving the integrity of both physical and digital components.

By systematically identifying the different document types and formats within your organization, you gain a comprehensive understanding of your document landscape. This knowledge forms the basis for developing targeted strategies and selecting appropriate technologies to effectively manage each document type. With a clear understanding of your document types, you can move forward in the document management journey, implementing solutions that optimize efficiency, accuracy, and compliance.

Determining Document Volume and Complexity

Assessing the volume and complexity of documents within your organization is a critical step in developing an effective document management strategy. Understanding the quantity, growth rate, and complexity of documents enables you to implement scalable and tailored solutions that can handle your organization's document management needs. This chapter focuses on guiding you through the process of determining document volume and complexity to facilitate better decision-making and optimize your document management practices.

1. Quantifying Document Volume: Document volume refers to the number of documents generated, received, and processed within your organization. Quantifying document volume helps you understand the scale of your document management needs and estimate resource requirements for handling them effectively. Consider the following aspects when determining document volume:

- Daily, Monthly, and Yearly Document Count: Assess the average number of documents created, received, and processed within specific timeframes. This provides a baseline for estimating the overall document volume.
- Document Sources: Identify the various sources of documents, such as departments, teams, external partners, customers, or suppliers. Each source may contribute differently to the overall document volume.
- Growth Rate: Analyze the growth rate of document volume over time. Consider factors such as business expansion, increasing customer base, or regulatory changes that may impact document generation and processing.
- Document Types: Classify documents based on their types and determine the volume of each type. This helps identify high-

volume document categories that may require specialized handling.

2. Assessing Document Complexity: Document complexity refers to the intricacy and variation within documents, which impacts the level of effort required for their management. Understanding document complexity enables you to design appropriate strategies for document processing, data extraction, and storage. Consider the following factors when assessing document complexity:

- Document Structures: Identify the presence of structured or unstructured documents. Structured documents follow a predefined format, often with standard fields, templates, or forms. Unstructured documents lack a consistent format or layout, making data extraction and processing more challenging.
- Data Extraction Requirements: Evaluate the complexity of data extraction from documents. Determine if documents contain specific data fields, such as customer information, transaction details, or product specifications. Assess whether the extraction requires manual entry, OCR technology, or advanced techniques like natural language processing (NLP).
- Document Variations: Analyze the variations in document formats, layouts, or versions. Determine if documents undergo frequent updates or revisions, leading to multiple versions or variations that need to be managed and tracked.
- Data Integration: Consider the need to integrate document data with other systems or applications. Assess whether data from documents needs to be transferred to customer relationship management (CRM) systems, enterprise resource planning (ERP) systems, or other databases for further processing or analysis.

- Data Security and Compliance: Evaluate the complexity of security and compliance requirements associated with documents. Determine if documents contain sensitive or confidential information that requires special handling, encryption, or access controls to ensure data protection and compliance with regulations.

3. Document Storage and Retrieval Considerations: Document volume and complexity directly impact storage and retrieval processes. Based on your assessment, consider the following considerations for effective storage and retrieval:

- Storage Capacity: Estimate the storage capacity required to accommodate the current document volume and anticipated growth. Determine whether on-premises or cloud-based solutions are suitable for your organization.
- Document Indexing: Assess the need for efficient document indexing to enable quick and accurate document retrieval. Identify the key data elements, metadata, or indexing criteria required for effective searching and filtering.
- Document Organization: Determine the optimal document organization structure, such as folders, categories, or tagging systems. Consider how documents can be logically organized to facilitate efficient retrieval based on different criteria (e.g., document type, date, or project).
- Search and Retrieval Speed: Assess the desired speed and responsiveness of document search and retrieval. Consider the need for advanced search capabilities, full-text search, or the ability to search within document content for more accurate results.

By determining document volume and complexity, you gain valuable insights into the scale of your document management needs. This information helps in selecting appropriate document management solutions, designing efficient workflows, and allocating resources effectively. With a comprehensive understanding of document volume and complexity, you can optimize your document management practices and lay the foundation for streamlined and scalable document processing and storage.

Analyzing Existing Document Management Processes

Analyzing your organization's existing document management processes is a crucial step in identifying areas for improvement and developing an effective document management strategy. By evaluating current practices, you can identify bottlenecks, inefficiencies, and pain points that hinder productivity, accuracy, and compliance. This chapter focuses on guiding you through the process of analyzing existing document management processes to identify opportunities for enhancement and optimization.

1. Document Workflow Assessment: A document workflow assessment involves mapping out the flow of documents within your organization from creation to storage and retrieval. Consider the following steps when analyzing your document workflows:

- Document Creation: Identify the processes and individuals responsible for document creation. Assess the efficiency of document creation workflows and determine if standardized templates or guidelines are in place.
- Review and Approval: Evaluate how documents undergo review and approval processes. Identify the stakeholders involved, the time taken for reviews, and any bottlenecks that delay the approval cycle.
- Document Distribution: Analyze how documents are distributed within your organization. Determine if the distribution methods (email, shared drives, cloud storage) are efficient and if there are any challenges in ensuring proper document access and version control.
- Document Storage and Organization: Assess how documents are stored, organized, and labeled within your existing document management systems. Consider the ease of document

retrieval, the presence of logical folder structures, and the consistency of document naming conventions.

- Document Archiving and Disposal: Evaluate the processes for archiving and disposing of documents that have reached the end of their lifecycle. Determine if there are policies and procedures in place to ensure compliance with data retention regulations and proper disposal of sensitive information.

2. Identification of Pain Points and Challenges: Identify pain points and challenges that hinder efficient document management. Common pain points include:

- Manual Data Entry: Assess the extent of manual data entry required for document processing. Determine if there are errors, delays, or inefficiencies resulting from manual data entry processes.
- Lack of Automation: Identify areas where automation can streamline document management processes. Consider tasks such as document classification, data extraction, and document routing that can be automated to improve efficiency.
- Inefficient Document Retrieval: Evaluate the challenges faced when retrieving documents, such as difficulty locating files, slow retrieval times, or limited search capabilities. Determine if these challenges impact productivity or customer service.
- Compliance and Security Risks: Analyze existing practices related to compliance and data security. Assess if there are risks of non-compliance with regulatory requirements, inadequate data protection measures, or vulnerabilities in document access controls.
- Lack of Collaboration: Assess the level of collaboration enabled by existing document management processes. Identify if there

are challenges in sharing documents, facilitating feedback, or maintaining version control when collaborating on documents.

- Technology Limitations: Evaluate the capabilities of current document management systems and technologies. Determine if they meet the evolving needs of your organization and if there are limitations impacting productivity, scalability, or integration with other systems.

3. Stakeholder Feedback and User Experience: Gather feedback from stakeholders involved in document management processes, including employees, managers, and customers. Conduct interviews, surveys, or focus groups to understand their experiences and pain points. Identify suggestions and recommendations for improving document management processes based on their insights.
4. Performance Metrics and Key Indicators: Establish performance metrics and key indicators to assess the effectiveness of existing document management processes. Consider metrics such as document processing time, accuracy of data extraction, document retrieval speed, compliance adherence, and customer satisfaction. By quantifying these metrics, you can track progress, identify areas for improvement, and measure the impact of implemented changes.
5. Gap Analysis and Improvement Opportunities: Based on the findings from the analysis, perform a gap analysis to identify areas for improvement. Compare existing practices against best practices, industry standards, and regulatory requirements. This analysis helps pinpoint gaps and opportunities for enhancement in document management processes, technologies, and policies.
6. Collaboration and Knowledge Sharing: Engage key stakeholders in collaborative discussions to share the findings of the analysis. Foster an environment where employees can provide insights, share best practices, and contribute ideas for improving document management processes. Encourage cross-

functional collaboration to ensure that perspectives from different departments are considered.

7. Documentation of Findings and Recommendations: Document the analysis findings and recommendations in a comprehensive report. Include a summary of pain points, challenges, opportunities, and suggested improvements. Prioritize the recommendations based on their potential impact and feasibility. This documentation serves as a valuable reference for developing your document management strategy and implementing the necessary changes.

By analyzing existing document management processes, you gain insights into areas that require improvement and optimization. This analysis serves as the foundation for developing a targeted document management strategy that addresses pain points, enhances efficiency, ensures compliance, and supports organizational goals.

Chapter 3: Creating an IDP Strategy

Overview: Creating an Intelligent Document Processing (IDP) strategy is a crucial step in leveraging AI and automation technologies to transform document-centric processes. In this chapter, we will guide you through the process of developing a comprehensive IDP strategy that aligns with your organization's goals, addresses specific document management challenges, and maximizes the benefits of IDP implementation. By creating a well-defined strategy, you can ensure a successful and effective integration of IDP into your document management practices.

1. Define Objectives and Goals: Begin by clearly defining your organization's objectives and goals for implementing IDP. Identify the specific outcomes you aim to achieve, such as improving efficiency, accuracy, compliance, or customer service. Ensure that your objectives align with the broader goals of your organization, and establish measurable key performance indicators (KPIs) to track progress and success.
2. Assess Current Document Management Practices: Evaluate your existing document management practices to understand the strengths, weaknesses, and gaps. Identify pain points, inefficiencies, and areas that can benefit from automation and AI. Assess the suitability of your current systems and processes for IDP implementation. This assessment serves as a foundation for designing an IDP strategy that addresses your organization's specific needs.
3. Identify Document Processes for Automation: Identify document-centric processes that can be automated using IDP. This includes tasks such as data extraction, document classification, validation, routing, and archival. Determine which processes can benefit most from automation in terms of time savings, accuracy improvement, and reduction of manual effort. Prioritize processes based on their impact on operational efficiency and strategic objectives.

4. Technology Selection: Evaluate available IDP technologies and solutions in the market. Consider factors such as their compatibility with your existing systems, scalability, ease of integration, and vendor support. Assess the capabilities of the IDP solution, such as machine learning algorithms, natural language processing, OCR, and data extraction accuracy. Choose a technology that aligns with your document management goals and requirements.
5. Data Security and Compliance: Ensure that your IDP strategy addresses data security and compliance requirements. Assess the sensitivity of the data processed through IDP and implement appropriate security measures to protect it. Consider compliance regulations related to data privacy, confidentiality, and retention. Choose an IDP solution that provides encryption, access controls, audit trails, and other security features to safeguard your documents and sensitive information.
6. Change Management and Training: Recognize the importance of change management and user adoption in successful IDP implementation. Develop a change management plan that includes communication, training, and support for employees who will be involved in IDP processes. Help users understand the benefits of IDP, provide training on the new technologies and processes, and address any concerns or resistance to change. A well-executed change management plan ensures a smooth transition and maximizes the benefits of IDP.
7. Pilot Testing and Iterative Implementation: Consider piloting IDP in a controlled environment or with a subset of documents and processes before full-scale implementation. This allows you to assess the effectiveness of the chosen IDP solution, make adjustments, and gather feedback from users. Use the insights gained from the pilot phase to refine your IDP strategy and ensure that it aligns with your organization's specific requirements.
8. Integration with Existing Systems: Ensure that your IDP strategy accounts for seamless integration with your existing systems and workflows. Identify integration points with other

applications, such as customer relationship management (CRM), enterprise resource planning (ERP), or content management systems. Smooth integration allows for data exchange, process automation, and unified document management across different systems.

9. Performance Monitoring and Continuous Improvement: Establish mechanisms to monitor the performance of your IDP implementation. Track KPIs related to efficiency, accuracy, cost savings, and user satisfaction. Continuously evaluate the impact of IDP on document management processes and make necessary adjustments for continuous improvement. Regularly review your IDP strategy to ensure it remains aligned with evolving business needs and technological advancements.

By creating a well-defined IDP strategy, you can ensure that your organization maximizes the benefits of AI and automation technologies in document management. A comprehensive strategy aligns with your organization's objectives, addresses specific challenges, and guides the successful implementation and integration of IDP into your document-centric processes.

Setting Clear Goals and Objectives

Setting clear goals and objectives is a critical step in creating a successful Intelligent Document Processing (IDP) strategy. Clear goals provide a direction for your IDP implementation and serve as benchmarks to measure success. In this section, we will delve into the details of setting clear goals and objectives for your IDP initiative.

1. Align Goals with Organizational Objectives: Start by aligning your IDP goals with your organization's broader objectives. Consider how IDP can contribute to improving operational efficiency, enhancing customer service, ensuring compliance, reducing costs, or driving innovation. By aligning IDP goals with organizational objectives, you ensure that your IDP strategy supports the overall mission and vision of the organization.

2. Be Specific and Measurable: Set goals that are specific and measurable to provide clarity and enable tracking of progress. Vague goals make it difficult to gauge success and determine if your IDP initiative is on track. For example, instead of stating a general goal like "improve efficiency," set a specific and measurable goal like "reduce document processing time by 30% within six months." This allows you to objectively measure the impact of your IDP implementation.
3. Consider Key Performance Indicators (KPIs): Identify key performance indicators (KPIs) that align with your goals and enable you to measure the success of your IDP initiative. KPIs should be quantifiable, meaningful, and directly linked to your objectives. Examples of relevant KPIs for IDP implementation include document processing time, accuracy of data extraction, cost savings, compliance adherence, or customer satisfaction ratings. Establish baseline measurements for these KPIs to track progress over time.
4. Make Goals Realistic and Attainable: Ensure that your goals are realistic and attainable based on your organization's resources, capabilities, and constraints. Setting overly ambitious goals that are not feasible can lead to frustration and potential failure. Assess your organization's current state, available resources, and technological readiness to determine what is realistically achievable within the desired timeframe.
5. Set Time-bound Targets: Set specific timeframes for achieving your IDP goals to create a sense of urgency and accountability. Establish short-term and long-term targets to provide milestones for tracking progress. For example, you may set a short-term target to automate data extraction for a specific document type within three months and a long-term target to achieve end-to-end automation for all document types within one year. Time-bound targets help prioritize tasks and ensure a structured implementation approach.
6. Communicate Goals Across the Organization: Communicate your IDP goals and objectives clearly across the organization to ensure alignment and foster a shared understanding of the

desired outcomes. Effective communication helps create buy-in from key stakeholders, including senior leadership, department heads, and employees involved in the IDP implementation. Clearly articulate the rationale behind the goals, the expected benefits, and the role each stakeholder plays in achieving them.

7. Foster Collaboration and Accountability: Encourage collaboration and foster a sense of ownership and accountability for achieving the IDP goals. Involve key stakeholders from different departments and functional areas in goal-setting discussions. Encourage cross-functional collaboration and establish mechanisms for ongoing communication and feedback. Assign responsibilities and define roles to ensure that individuals and teams understand their contributions towards achieving the IDP objectives.
8. Regularly Review and Update Goals: Regularly review and update your IDP goals to ensure their relevance and alignment with evolving business needs. Document management requirements and priorities may change over time, and your goals should reflect these changes. Conduct periodic assessments to determine if goals are being met, identify areas for improvement, and make necessary adjustments to your IDP strategy.

By setting clear goals and objectives, you provide a roadmap for your IDP implementation. Clear goals help guide decision-making, prioritize tasks, and measure success. Ensure that your goals align with organizational objectives, are specific and measurable, realistic and attainable, time-bound, and communicated effectively. With well-defined goals, you can drive your IDP initiative towards success and achieve the desired benefits in document management and automation.

Selecting the Right IDP Solution

Selecting the right Intelligent Document Processing (IDP) solution is crucial for the success of your document management initiative. The IDP solution you choose should align with your organization's goals, meet your specific requirements, and effectively address your document processing challenges. In this section, we will explore the key factors to consider when selecting an IDP solution.

1. Assess Document Management Needs: Before selecting an IDP solution, thoroughly assess your document management needs. Identify the specific challenges you aim to address through IDP, such as manual data entry, inefficient document retrieval, or compliance issues. Determine the types of documents you handle, their volume, complexity, and the desired outcomes you expect from the IDP solution. This assessment serves as a foundation for identifying the features and functionalities required in an IDP solution.
2. Compatibility and Integration: Evaluate the compatibility and integration capabilities of the IDP solution with your existing systems and workflows. Ensure that the solution can seamlessly integrate with your document management systems, enterprise applications, or other software platforms. This enables efficient data exchange, automated workflows, and unified document management across different systems. Consider the ease of integration, the availability of APIs, and the compatibility with your technology infrastructure.
3. Automation Capabilities: An effective IDP solution should offer robust automation capabilities. Evaluate the automation features provided by the solution, such as document classification, data extraction, validation, and routing. Consider the accuracy of the automation algorithms and the ability of the solution to learn and improve over time through machine learning techniques. The solution should streamline document-centric processes, reduce manual effort, and enhance operational efficiency.
4. Data Extraction Accuracy and Flexibility: Accurate data extraction is a critical aspect of IDP. Assess the solution's ability to accurately extract data from various document types and formats, including both structured and unstructured documents. Consider the flexibility of the solution in adapting to different layouts, variations, and languages. Look for features such as

optical character recognition (OCR), natural language processing (NLP), and the capability to validate extracted data against predefined rules or databases.

5. Scalability and Performance: Consider the scalability and performance capabilities of the IDP solution. Evaluate its ability to handle large volumes of documents efficiently without compromising performance. Determine if the solution can scale as your organization grows and document volumes increase. Look for features such as distributed processing, parallel computing, and efficient resource utilization to ensure that the solution can accommodate your future needs.
6. Security and Compliance: Ensure that the IDP solution meets your organization's security and compliance requirements. Assess the solution's security features, including data encryption, access controls, user authentication, and audit trails. Verify if the solution complies with relevant data privacy regulations, industry standards, and security best practices. Consider any specific compliance requirements related to your industry or organization, such as HIPAA for healthcare or GDPR for data protection.
7. User Experience and Interface: Evaluate the user experience and interface of the IDP solution. A user-friendly interface simplifies document processing tasks and reduces the learning curve for employees. Consider the intuitiveness of the solution's interface, ease of use, and availability of features like drag-and-drop functionality or customizable workflows. The solution should empower users to efficiently interact with documents, validate data, and collaborate seamlessly.
8. Vendor Support and Reputation: Assess the reputation and track record of the IDP solution vendor. Research customer reviews, case studies, and testimonials to gauge the vendor's reliability, customer support, and commitment to ongoing product enhancements. Consider the vendor's expertise in the field of document management, their responsiveness to support requests, and their ability to provide timely updates and bug fixes.

9. Total Cost of Ownership (TCO): Evaluate the total cost of ownership (TCO) associated with implementing the IDP solution. Consider not only the initial licensing or subscription costs but also factors like implementation, training, customization, ongoing support, and maintenance. Assess the long-term value and return on investment (ROI) the solution can provide, considering the potential cost savings, efficiency gains, and other benefits.
10. Proof of Concept (POC) and Piloting: Consider conducting a proof of concept (POC) or piloting the IDP solution before making a full-scale implementation. This allows you to evaluate the solution's performance, accuracy, and compatibility with your specific document management needs. A POC helps validate the solution's capabilities and assess its suitability for your organization, enabling you to make an informed decision.

By carefully evaluating these factors, you can select an IDP solution that best aligns with your organization's goals and requirements. A well-chosen IDP solution can streamline document processing, improve efficiency, accuracy, and compliance, and contribute to the overall success of your document management initiative.

Defining Key Performance Indicators (KPIs)

Defining key performance indicators (KPIs) is crucial for measuring the success and effectiveness of your Intelligent Document Processing (IDP) implementation. KPIs provide measurable metrics that align with your organization's goals and objectives. By establishing clear KPIs, you can track progress, identify areas for improvement, and demonstrate the impact of IDP on your document management processes. In this section, we will explore the details of defining KPIs for your IDP initiative.

1. Align KPIs with Objectives: Ensure that your KPIs directly align with the objectives and goals of your IDP initiative. Each KPI should contribute to measuring the success of specific aspects of your document management processes. For example, if one of your objectives is to improve efficiency, a relevant KPI

could be "reduction in document processing time" or "increase in the number of documents processed per hour."

2. Make KPIs Specific and Measurable: KPIs should be specific and measurable to provide clarity and enable tracking of progress. Avoid vague or subjective KPIs that are difficult to quantify or evaluate. Ensure that each KPI has a clear numerical value or target that can be objectively measured. For example, a specific and measurable KPI could be "achieving a 20% reduction in manual data entry errors."
3. Consider Multiple Dimensions: Consider different dimensions of your document management processes when defining KPIs. This allows you to capture a comprehensive view of your IDP implementation. Common dimensions to consider include efficiency, accuracy, compliance, customer satisfaction, and cost savings. Each dimension may have its own set of KPIs that reflect the specific goals and requirements related to that dimension.
4. Quantitative and Qualitative KPIs: Balance your KPIs between quantitative and qualitative measures to capture both objective and subjective aspects of your IDP implementation. While quantitative KPIs provide measurable metrics, qualitative KPIs help gauge user satisfaction, perception, and overall experience. For example, a quantitative KPI could be "reduction in document retrieval time," while a qualitative KPI could be "improvement in user satisfaction with document search capabilities."
5. Establish Baseline Measurements: Establish baseline measurements for your KPIs to provide a starting point for comparison and progress tracking. Baseline measurements represent the current state of your document management processes before implementing IDP. By comparing future measurements against the baseline, you can assess the impact and effectiveness of your IDP implementation.
6. Define Target Values and Timeframes: Set target values for each KPI to establish the desired level of performance or improvement. Target values provide a clear goal for your IDP

initiative and enable you to measure progress. Additionally, define timeframes for achieving these targets to create a sense of urgency and accountability. Time-bound targets help prioritize tasks and ensure a structured approach to IDP implementation.

7. Ensure Actionability: Ensure that your KPIs are actionable, meaning they provide insights that can drive meaningful actions and improvements. Each KPI should highlight specific areas where changes can be made to enhance document management processes. For example, if a KPI shows a high error rate in data extraction, it prompts action to review and improve the data extraction models or algorithms.
8. Regular Monitoring and Reporting: Regularly monitor and track the KPIs to measure progress and identify trends. Establish a reporting mechanism to provide periodic updates on the performance of your IDP implementation. Regular monitoring allows you to make timely adjustments, address any issues, and demonstrate the value of IDP to stakeholders.
9. Continuously Review and Update KPIs: Review and update your KPIs periodically to ensure their relevance and alignment with evolving business needs. As your document management processes mature and change, your KPIs may need to be revised or expanded. Regularly assess the effectiveness of existing KPIs and consider adding new ones to capture emerging requirements or areas of focus.

By defining clear and relevant KPIs for your IDP implementation, you gain valuable insights into the impact of IDP on your document management processes. KPIs enable you to track progress, measure success, identify areas for improvement, and demonstrate the value of IDP to stakeholders throughout your organization.

CHAPTER 4: PREPARING YOUR DOCUMENTS FOR IDP

Overview: Preparing your documents for Intelligent Document Processing (IDP) is a crucial step in ensuring successful and accurate automation. This chapter focuses on guiding you through the process of organizing, structuring, and optimizing your documents to maximize the effectiveness of IDP technologies. By preparing your documents effectively, you can streamline the document processing workflow, enhance data extraction accuracy, and improve overall efficiency in your IDP implementation.

1. Document Classification and Categorization: Start by classifying and categorizing your documents based on their types, formats, and content. Identify common document categories, such as invoices, purchase orders, contracts, or customer forms. This allows you to establish a framework for organizing and processing documents efficiently. Classifying documents also helps in determining the specific IDP techniques or models that are suitable for each document type.
2. Standardizing Document Formats: Standardize document formats to ensure consistency and ease of processing. Establish guidelines for document layout, structure, and formatting. This includes defining templates, using consistent fonts and font sizes, establishing standardized field placements, and ensuring a uniform structure across documents of the same type. Standardization facilitates automated data extraction and reduces the complexity of IDP implementation.
3. Data Extraction Fields and Markers: Identify and define the specific data extraction fields and markers within your documents. These fields represent the key pieces of information that need to be extracted accurately by the IDP solution. Examples of data extraction fields include customer names, addresses, invoice numbers, or product descriptions. By clearly

defining these fields, you enable the IDP solution to focus on extracting the relevant information and reduce the chances of errors or missing data.

4. Pre-processing and Quality Assurance: Perform pre-processing tasks to optimize your documents for IDP. This may involve tasks such as image enhancement, noise reduction, or resolution adjustments for scanned documents. Additionally, implement quality assurance measures to ensure the integrity and accuracy of the document data. Validate the extracted data against predefined rules, perform data validations, and implement mechanisms for detecting and resolving errors or inconsistencies.
5. Document Version Control: Establish a document version control system to manage changes and revisions. Implement mechanisms to track and store different document versions, including updates, edits, or annotations. This ensures that the IDP solution can process the most recent and accurate version of the document. Document version control helps maintain data integrity, reduce confusion, and prevent errors resulting from outdated information.
6. Metadata and Indexing: Implement metadata and indexing strategies to enhance document search and retrieval. Metadata includes additional information about documents, such as keywords, tags, or descriptions, which facilitate efficient searching and filtering. Indexing involves organizing documents based on specific criteria, such as document type, date, or project, to enable quick and accurate retrieval. Proper metadata and indexing enable smooth navigation and improve the overall document management experience.
7. Document Security and Access Controls: Consider document security and access controls when preparing your documents for IDP. Determine the appropriate level of access and permissions for different users or roles involved in the document management process. Implement security measures to protect sensitive or confidential information, such as encryption, authentication protocols, or secure storage solutions.

Maintaining proper document security ensures data privacy, compliance with regulations, and mitigates the risk of unauthorized access.

8. Document Retention and Disposal: Establish document retention and disposal policies to manage the lifecycle of your documents. Determine the appropriate duration for retaining documents based on legal and regulatory requirements. Implement processes for archiving documents that need to be retained and define protocols for secure disposal of documents that have reached the end of their lifecycle. Proper document retention and disposal practices promote compliance, reduce storage costs, and streamline document management processes.

By effectively preparing your documents for IDP, you create a solid foundation for accurate and efficient automation. Organizing, structuring, and optimizing your documents ensure that the IDP solution can effectively process and extract information from them. Implementing document classification, standardization, data extraction fields, quality assurance measures, and document security measures contribute to the overall success of your IDP implementation.

Standardizing Document Formats and Layouts

Standardizing document formats and layouts is a crucial step in preparing your documents for Intelligent Document Processing (IDP). By establishing consistent formats and layouts, you enable the IDP solution to accurately process and extract information from your documents. In this section, we will explore the details of standardizing document formats and layouts for effective IDP implementation.

1. Define Document Templates: Start by defining document templates for different document types within your organization. Document templates serve as a blueprint that establishes the structure, layout, and formatting guidelines for specific document categories. Templates provide a consistent framework for document creation and processing, reducing variations and ensuring uniformity across documents of the same type.
2. Layout Design: Design document layouts that are user-friendly and optimized for IDP. Consider the following aspects when designing the layout:

a. Clear Sections: Organize the document into clear sections such as headers, footers, body, and sidebars. Clearly demarcate each section to enable easy identification and extraction of relevant information by the IDP solution.

b. Logical Flow: Ensure that the layout follows a logical flow, guiding the reader through the document in a structured manner. Arrange information in a logical sequence, considering the expected reading order or user attention flow.

c. Consistent Field Placement: Maintain consistency in the placement of fields or data elements across document instances. For example, if an invoice always has the invoice date in the top right corner, ensure that this field is consistently placed in the same location across all invoices.

d. White Space Management: Optimize the use of white space to enhance readability and reduce clutter. Well-managed white space improves the accuracy of automated text extraction and allows the IDP solution to focus on extracting relevant information.

e. Font and Formatting: Select legible fonts and font sizes to ensure readability. Consistently apply font styles, such as bold or italic, to indicate specific information. Use font formatting consistently across documents to facilitate accurate data extraction.

f. Headers and Footers: Include standardized headers and footers that provide relevant information such as document title, date, page numbers, or company logos. Consistent headers and footers enhance document identification and maintain a professional appearance.

3. Data Field Labeling: Clearly label data fields within the document layout to indicate the type of information they represent. For example, label fields such as "Invoice Number," "Customer Name," or "Due Date" to provide explicit instructions for the IDP solution. Clearly labeled fields improve the accuracy of data extraction and reduce the chances of errors or misinterpretation.
4. Document Orientation and Page Size: Maintain consistent document orientation (e.g., portrait or landscape) and page sizes for documents of the same type. Consistent orientation and page sizes contribute to the overall visual coherence and facilitate automated processing by the IDP solution. Avoid variations in orientation or page sizes, as they may introduce complexities during document scanning, extraction, or storage.
5. Handling Variations: While standardizing document formats and layouts, consider the potential variations that may exist within a document type. Some documents may have unique sections, optional fields, or specific formatting requirements. Define guidelines or rules to handle these variations, ensuring that the IDP solution can handle them accurately.
6. Version Control: Implement a version control system to manage updates or changes to document templates. Maintain a central repository for document templates, ensuring that the latest versions are readily accessible to users. Clearly communicate

version control procedures and guidelines to relevant stakeholders to avoid confusion and discrepancies.

7. User Feedback and Iterative Improvement: Seek feedback from users who handle the documents regularly. Their insights can help identify areas where standardization can be improved or where adjustments may be necessary. Iterate on the document templates based on user feedback, emerging requirements, or changes in document management processes.

By standardizing document formats and layouts, you create a consistent structure and visual representation that facilitates efficient document processing by IDP solutions. Consistency in formats and layouts enhances the accuracy of data extraction, improves automation capabilities, and streamlines the overall document management process.

Optimizing Image Quality and Resolution

Optimizing the quality and resolution of images is an important aspect of preparing your documents for Intelligent Document Processing (IDP). Clear and high-quality images ensure accurate data extraction and enhance the overall performance of IDP solutions. In this section, we will delve into the details of optimizing image quality and resolution for effective IDP implementation.

1. Image Enhancement Techniques: Apply image enhancement techniques to improve the quality of scanned or captured images. These techniques can help address common issues such as blurriness, noise, or low contrast. Consider the following image enhancement techniques:

a. De-skewing: Correct skew or rotation in scanned documents to align them properly.

b. De-noising: Reduce noise or graininess in the image caused by scanning or poor lighting conditions.

c. Contrast Enhancement: Adjust contrast levels to ensure that text and other important details are clearly visible.

d. Brightness and Gamma Correction: Optimize brightness and gamma levels to enhance image clarity.

e. Edge Enhancement: Sharpen image edges to improve text legibility and image quality.

f. Background Removal: Remove unnecessary background elements to reduce distractions and improve data extraction accuracy.

2. Image Resolution: Ensure that the image resolution is suitable for accurate data extraction. Higher resolutions generally provide better quality and enable improved text recognition. Consider the following factors when determining the optimal image resolution:

a. DPI (Dots Per Inch): DPI refers to the number of dots or pixels per inch in an image. Higher DPI values generally result in clearer and more detailed images. For text-based documents, a resolution of 300 DPI is typically sufficient for accurate data extraction.

b. Scanning Parameters: If you are scanning physical documents, adjust scanning settings to capture images at an appropriate resolution. Refer to the scanner's specifications and guidelines for optimal scanning resolutions.

c. Image Compression: Avoid excessive image compression that can degrade image quality. Ensure that the compression settings balance file size with image quality to maintain readability and accuracy.

3. Image File Format: Select an appropriate file format that balances image quality, file size, and compatibility. Common image file formats for IDP include JPEG, PNG, and TIFF. Consider the following aspects when choosing an image file format:

a. Compression: Evaluate the compression capabilities of the file format. Opt for formats that support lossless compression or provide a good balance between compression and image quality.

b. Compatibility: Ensure that the selected file format is compatible with your IDP solution and other software, or systems involved in the document processing workflow.

c. Metadata Support: Check if the file format supports embedding metadata or additional information about the image. Metadata can be helpful for indexing, searching, and identifying images during the IDP process.

4. Quality Assurance and Validation: Implement quality assurance measures to validate the image quality and accuracy of data extraction. Set up procedures to review and verify the images processed by the IDP solution. Perform regular quality checks to ensure that images meet the required standards for accurate data extraction.
5. Retention of Original Images: Retain the original high-quality images alongside the processed data to support validation, audit,

or compliance requirements. Archiving the original images allows for future reference and ensures the availability of source material if reprocessing is necessary.

6. Image Storage Considerations: Determine the storage requirements for images based on their resolution and file format. Assess the storage capacity needed to accommodate the volume of images generated and processed by your IDP solution. Consider both on-premises and cloud storage options, ensuring that images are easily accessible, secure, and backed up regularly.

By optimizing the quality and resolution of images, you improve the accuracy of data extraction and enhance the performance of your IDP solution. High-quality images reduce errors, facilitate efficient text recognition, and contribute to the overall success of your document management processes.

Implementing Document Classification and Indexing

Implementing document classification and indexing is a critical step in organizing and managing your documents effectively for Intelligent Document Processing (IDP). Document classification involves categorizing documents into specific types or classes, while indexing involves assigning metadata or tags to enable quick and accurate document retrieval. In this section, we will explore the details of implementing document classification and indexing for successful IDP implementation.

1. Define Document Types and Classes: Start by defining the document types and classes relevant to your organization. Document types may include invoices, contracts, purchase orders, customer forms, or any other document categories specific to your industry or business processes. Determine the attributes or characteristics that distinguish each document type. This information forms the basis for classification and subsequent processing by the IDP solution.
2. Document Classification Techniques: Consider different document classification techniques to automate the categorization process. These techniques include rule-based classification, keyword-based classification, or machine learning-based classification. Rule-based classification involves defining specific rules or conditions to assign documents to classes based on predefined criteria. Keyword-based classification involves matching documents against a predefined set of keywords or phrases. Machine learning-based classification involves training algorithms using labeled documents to automatically classify new documents. Determine the most suitable technique(s) based on your document complexity, volume, and available resources.
3. Metadata and Indexing Criteria: Define the metadata and indexing criteria for your documents. Metadata provides additional information about the documents, facilitating accurate indexing and searchability. Determine the relevant

metadata fields for each document type, such as document title, author, date, client name, or project ID. Define the format and structure of the metadata fields to ensure consistency and ease of retrieval. Consider the specific indexing criteria that will be used to tag documents, such as document type, date, customer name, or any other relevant attributes.

4. Automated Document Classification: Leverage IDP technologies to automate document classification. Train the IDP solution using labeled documents to enable machine learning algorithms to recognize patterns and classify new documents accurately. Utilize techniques such as natural language processing (NLP) or text mining to extract key features or characteristics for classification. Continuously evaluate and refine the automated classification models to improve accuracy and adapt to changing document patterns.
5. Manual Document Classification: In cases where automated classification may not be feasible or sufficient, employ manual document classification. Assign trained personnel to review and classify documents based on predetermined criteria. Develop clear guidelines and instructions for manual classification to ensure consistency and accuracy. Consider establishing a validation process to verify the accuracy of automated classification results and make necessary adjustments.
6. Indexing and Metadata Application: Apply the defined metadata fields and indexing criteria to documents. Capture the relevant information for each document and populate the metadata fields accordingly. This step may involve data entry, extraction from document content, or integration with external systems. Ensure consistency and accuracy when assigning metadata to enable efficient document retrieval and search functionality.
7. Document Repository and Storage: Establish a centralized document repository or database to store classified and indexed documents. Choose a storage solution that supports efficient indexing, search, and retrieval capabilities. Organize the repository based on document types, classes, or other relevant criteria. Implement version control mechanisms to manage

revisions and updates, ensuring that the latest versions are readily accessible.

8. Search and Retrieval Capabilities: Implement robust search and retrieval capabilities to facilitate quick and accurate document retrieval. Develop an intuitive user interface that allows users to search documents based on metadata fields, keywords, or document attributes. Incorporate advanced search features such as full-text search, fuzzy search, or faceted search to enhance user experience and accessibility.
9. Continuous Improvement: Regularly review and evaluate the effectiveness of document classification and indexing processes. Collect feedback from users and stakeholders to identify areas for improvement. Monitor the accuracy of document classification results and adjust the models or criteria, as necessary. Continuously refine your classification and indexing strategies to enhance the efficiency and accuracy of document management processes.

By implementing document classification and indexing, you establish a systematic approach to organizing and retrieving documents, enabling efficient document processing by IDP solutions. Proper classification and indexing enhance data extraction accuracy, streamline document retrieval, and contribute to the overall success of your IDP implementation.

CHAPTER 5: CHOOSING THE RIGHT IDP SOLUTION

Overview: Choosing the right Intelligent Document Processing (IDP) solution is crucial for the success of your document management initiative. With a wide range of IDP solutions available in the market, selecting the one that aligns with your organization's specific needs and requirements can be a complex task. In this chapter, we will provide guidance on how to choose the right IDP solution by considering various factors such as functionality, scalability, integration capabilities, vendor support, and cost. Making an informed decision in selecting the right IDP solution will help ensure a seamless implementation and maximize the benefits of automation in your document management processes.

1. Assess Your Document Management Needs: Begin by assessing your organization's document management needs. Identify the specific challenges and pain points you want to address through IDP. Consider factors such as the volume and complexity of your documents, the desired automation capabilities, and the expected outcomes. This assessment will serve as a foundation for understanding your requirements and selecting an IDP solution that can effectively meet those needs.
2. Define Key Functionality Requirements: Define the key functionality requirements that your IDP solution should have. Consider features such as document classification, data extraction, validation, workflow automation, integration capabilities, and reporting. Determine which functionalities are essential for your document management processes and prioritize them based on their importance and potential impact on efficiency and accuracy.
3. Scalability and Performance: Evaluate the scalability and performance capabilities of the IDP solution. Assess its ability to handle a growing volume of documents and increasing processing demands. Consider factors such as distributed

processing, parallel computing, and resource utilization to ensure that the solution can scale effectively as your document management needs expand. Performance is crucial to ensure efficient processing and timely results.

4. Integration with Existing Systems: Consider the integration capabilities of the IDP solution with your existing systems and workflows. Evaluate whether the solution can seamlessly integrate with your document management systems, enterprise resource planning (ERP) systems, customer relationship management (CRM) systems, or other relevant software applications. Smooth integration enables data exchange, process automation, and unified document management across different systems, reducing manual effort and enhancing overall efficiency.
5. Vendor Support and Reputation: Evaluate the vendor's support and reputation. Research the vendor's track record, customer reviews, case studies, and testimonials to assess their reliability, customer support, and commitment to ongoing product enhancements. Consider factors such as responsiveness to support requests, software updates, and bug fixes. A reputable vendor with a strong support system ensures a smooth implementation and reliable ongoing support for your IDP solution.
6. Technology and Innovation: Assess the technological capabilities and innovation of the IDP solution. Consider factors such as the adoption of artificial intelligence (AI) and machine learning (ML) technologies, natural language processing (NLP) capabilities, optical character recognition (OCR) accuracy, and the ability to adapt and improve over time. A technologically advanced solution can provide better accuracy, efficiency, and adaptability to changing document management requirements.
7. Security and Compliance: Ensure that the IDP solution meets your organization's security and compliance requirements. Evaluate the solution's security features, including data encryption, access controls, user authentication, and audit trails. Verify if the solution complies with relevant data privacy

regulations, industry standards, and security best practices. Consider any specific compliance requirements related to your industry or organization, such as HIPAA for healthcare or GDPR for data protection.

8. Total Cost of Ownership (TCO): Evaluate the total cost of ownership (TCO) associated with the IDP solution. Consider not only the initial licensing or subscription costs but also factors such as implementation, training, customization, ongoing support, and maintenance. Assess the long-term value and return on investment (ROI) the solution can provide, considering the potential cost savings, efficiency gains, and other benefits it offers.
9. Proof of Concept (POC) and Piloting: Consider conducting a proof of concept (POC) or piloting the IDP solution before making a full-scale implementation. A POC allows you to assess the solution's performance, accuracy, and compatibility with your specific document management needs. It also provides an opportunity to evaluate the user experience and gather feedback from key stakeholders. A POC helps validate the solution's capabilities and ensures its suitability for your organization.

By considering these factors and conducting a thorough evaluation, you can select the right IDP solution that aligns with your organization's needs, ensures seamless integration, and maximizes the benefits of automation in your document management processes. Choosing the right IDP solution sets the stage for a successful implementation and supports your organization's digital transformation journey.

Exploring OCR (Optical Character Recognition) Technologies

OCR (Optical Character Recognition) technologies play a crucial role in Intelligent Document Processing (IDP) by enabling the extraction of text and data from scanned or digital documents. OCR technologies convert images of text into machine-readable text, facilitating automated document processing and analysis. In this section, we will delve into the details of

OCR technologies, their benefits, and considerations when exploring OCR for your IDP implementation.

1. How OCR Works: OCR technologies use image processing techniques and machine learning algorithms to recognize and extract text from images. The OCR process typically involves the following steps:

a. Image Preprocessing: Preprocessing techniques are applied to enhance the quality of the document image, such as de-skewing, de-noising, or contrast adjustment.

b. Text Localization: OCR algorithms identify and locate areas in the image that contain text, distinguishing text from other elements such as images or graphics.

c. Character Recognition: OCR algorithms analyze the text regions and attempt to recognize individual characters by comparing them against a trained character database or statistical models.

d. Text Segmentation: Recognized characters are grouped together to form words, sentences, and paragraphs, replicating the original document's structure.

e. Post-processing: Additional techniques, such as spell-checking, language modeling, or context analysis, may be applied to improve the accuracy and usability of the extracted text.

2. Benefits of OCR Technologies: OCR technologies offer several benefits in the context of IDP:

a. Data Extraction: OCR enables the extraction of text and data from scanned or digital documents, automating the process that would otherwise require manual data entry.

b. Accuracy and Efficiency: OCR technologies have significantly improved in accuracy and speed, leading to higher efficiency in document processing and reducing human errors.

c. Document Searchability: By converting image-based documents into searchable text, OCR enables quick and accurate document retrieval based on specific keywords or phrases.

d. Automation and Workflow Integration: OCR technologies integrate seamlessly with document management systems and workflows, enabling automated processing, routing, and archiving of documents.

e. Data Analysis and Insights: Extracted text can be further analyzed using natural language processing (NLP) and machine learning techniques, enabling advanced data analysis and extraction of meaningful insights.

3. Considerations when Exploring OCR: When exploring OCR technologies for your IDP implementation, consider the following factors:

a. Accuracy and Language Support: Evaluate the accuracy of the OCR technology in recognizing different fonts, languages, and document layouts. Verify its support for multilingual documents or specific character sets relevant to your organization.

b. Document Complexity: Assess how well the OCR technology handles complex documents, such as those with tables, images, or handwritten sections. Some OCR solutions excel in specific document types, while others offer more versatility.

c. Integration Capabilities: Ensure that the OCR solution can seamlessly integrate with your existing document management systems, IDP platforms, or other software applications involved in the document processing workflow.

d. Scalability: Consider the scalability of the OCR technology, particularly if you anticipate increasing document volumes or processing demands in the future. The OCR solution should accommodate your organization's growth without compromising performance.

e. OCR Training and Customization: Evaluate the ability to train and customize the OCR solution to meet specific document types or requirements unique to your organization. This may include adjusting recognition parameters, adding custom dictionaries, or training models for specific fonts or layouts.

f. OCR Confidence and Validation: Understand the OCR solution's confidence levels in recognizing characters or words. Implement validation processes to verify and ensure the accuracy of the extracted text, particularly for critical or sensitive information.

g. Security and Compliance: Assess the OCR solution's security features, data privacy measures, and compliance with relevant regulations (e.g., GDPR, HIPAA) to protect sensitive information during the OCR process.

h. Vendor Support and Updates: Consider the vendor's reputation, track record, and customer support. Evaluate the frequency of updates, bug fixes, and their responsiveness to support requests.

4. Combination with Machine Learning and AI: OCR technologies can be enhanced through the integration of machine learning and AI techniques. By training OCR models with large datasets and implementing advanced algorithms, OCR solutions can adapt to various document layouts, improve accuracy, and handle more complex document types. Consider OCR solutions that incorporate machine learning and AI for enhanced performance and accuracy.

OCR technologies are essential components of IDP, enabling efficient data extraction and automation in document processing. By exploring OCR options and considering the relevant factors, you can select an OCR solution that best suits your organization's needs, enhances accuracy, and streamlines your document management processes.

Understanding Machine Learning and Natural Language Processing

Machine Learning (ML) and Natural Language Processing (NLP) are two key technologies that play a significant role in Intelligent Document Processing (IDP). ML enables computers to learn from data and make predictions or decisions without explicit programming, while NLP focuses on the interaction between computers and human language. In this section, we will explore the details of machine learning and natural language processing and their relevance in IDP.

1. Machine Learning (ML): Machine Learning is a subset of artificial intelligence (AI) that focuses on algorithms and statistical models that enable computers to learn from data and improve performance on specific tasks. ML algorithms can be broadly categorized into supervised learning, unsupervised learning, and reinforcement learning:

a. Supervised Learning: In supervised learning, models are trained on labeled data, where inputs and desired outputs are provided. The models learn patterns from the data and make predictions on unseen data based on the learned patterns.

b. Unsupervised Learning: Unsupervised learning involves training models on unlabeled data, where no specific outputs are provided. The models identify patterns or structures in the data without prior knowledge of the expected outcomes.

c. Reinforcement Learning: Reinforcement learning involves training models to interact with an environment and learn from feedback in the form of rewards or penalties. The models make decisions based on maximizing cumulative rewards.

ML techniques are relevant to IDP in various ways:

a. Document Classification: ML models can be trained to classify documents into different categories or types, enabling automated document sorting and routing.

b. Data Extraction: ML algorithms can learn patterns in document layouts and structures to extract relevant data such as names, addresses, or invoice amounts. These models can adapt to variations in document formats, improving accuracy and efficiency in data extraction.

c. Document Clustering: ML models can analyze the content and characteristics of documents to group similar documents together, aiding in document organization and retrieval.

d. Anomaly Detection: ML algorithms can identify anomalies or irregularities in document content or behavior, helping detect fraudulent activities or errors in document processing.

e. Continuous Improvement: ML models can be trained iteratively with new data to improve performance over time. This allows the models to adapt to evolving document patterns and optimize accuracy in IDP.

2. Natural Language Processing (NLP): Natural Language Processing is a field of AI that focuses on the interaction between computers and human language. NLP techniques enable computers to understand, interpret, and generate human language in a meaningful way. NLP encompasses various tasks such as:

a. Text Classification: NLP models can classify text documents based on their content, sentiment, or topic. This aids in document organization and analysis.

b. Named Entity Recognition (NER): NER involves identifying and extracting named entities such as person names, organizations, or locations from text. NER models are useful in extracting key information from documents.

c. Sentiment Analysis: Sentiment analysis techniques determine the sentiment or opinion expressed in text, helping assess customer feedback or sentiment in documents.

d. Language Generation: NLP models can generate human-like text, enabling the automation of tasks such as report generation or content creation.

e. Machine Translation: NLP models facilitate automated translation of text from one language to another, aiding in multilingual document processing.

NLP techniques are essential in IDP as they enable the understanding, interpretation, and processing of textual information in documents. By utilizing NLP, IDP solutions can extract meaning, sentiment, and key entities from text, enhancing data extraction accuracy and enabling advanced document analysis.

3. Integration of ML and NLP in IDP: ML and NLP techniques are often combined in IDP to enhance document processing capabilities. ML models can learn from labeled data to improve

the accuracy of NLP tasks such as text classification, sentiment analysis, or entity recognition. Additionally, NLP techniques can be applied to textual data extracted through ML-based data extraction, enabling further analysis and insights.

The integration of ML and NLP in IDP empowers organizations to automate document processing tasks, extract meaningful information, and gain valuable insights from textual data. Leveraging these technologies helps streamline document management, improve efficiency, and enable more sophisticated analysis of document content.

Evaluating IDP Software Providers

Choosing the right Intelligent Document Processing (IDP) software provider is a critical decision that can significantly impact the success of your document management initiatives. As IDP continues to evolve, numerous software providers offer solutions with varying capabilities, features, and support. To ensure you make an informed decision, it is important to evaluate IDP software providers based on several key factors. In this section, we will explore the details of evaluating IDP software providers.

1. Technology and Features: Assess the technology stack and features offered by the IDP software provider. Consider whether the solution aligns with your specific document management needs, such as document classification, data extraction, validation, workflow automation, or integration capabilities. Evaluate the software's ability to handle various document formats, complexity levels, and languages. Additionally, consider any unique features or innovations offered by the provider that can address your specific requirements.
2. Scalability and Performance: Evaluate the scalability and performance capabilities of the IDP software. Consider the software's ability to handle increasing document volumes, high processing demands, and simultaneous user access. Assess the performance metrics, such as processing speed, accuracy rates, and resource utilization, to ensure the solution can meet your organization's current and future requirements.
3. Integration Capabilities: Determine the integration capabilities of the IDP software provider. Evaluate whether the solution can seamlessly integrate with your existing systems and workflows, including document management systems, enterprise resource planning (ERP) systems, customer relationship management (CRM) systems, or other relevant software applications. Smooth integration enables data exchange, process automation, and

unified document management across different systems, reducing manual effort and enhancing overall efficiency.

4. Vendor Support and Reputation: Evaluate the vendor's support and reputation. Research the vendor's track record, customer reviews, case studies, and testimonials to assess their reliability, customer support, and commitment to ongoing product enhancements. Consider the responsiveness of the vendor to support requests, the frequency of software updates, and the quality of bug fixes. A reputable vendor with a strong support system ensures a smooth implementation and reliable ongoing support for your IDP solution.
5. Security and Compliance: Assess the security measures and compliance standards followed by the IDP software provider. Consider whether the solution provides robust security features, such as data encryption, access controls, user authentication, and audit trails. Verify if the software complies with relevant data privacy regulations, industry standards, and security best practices. Evaluate the provider's commitment to data security, protection of sensitive information, and adherence to compliance requirements specific to your industry or organization.
6. Cost and Pricing Model: Evaluate the cost and pricing model of the IDP software. Consider the initial licensing or subscription costs, as well as any additional fees or charges, such as implementation, training, customization, ongoing support, or maintenance costs. Assess the long-term value and return on investment (ROI) the solution can provide, considering the potential cost savings, efficiency gains, and other benefits it offers. Ensure transparency in pricing and understand any limitations or restrictions associated with the pricing model.
7. Proof of Concept (POC) and References: Consider requesting a proof of concept (POC) from the IDP software provider. A POC allows you to test the solution's performance, accuracy, and suitability for your specific document management needs. It provides an opportunity to evaluate the user experience and gather feedback from key stakeholders. Additionally, ask the

software provider for references or case studies from organizations similar to yours to validate the solution's effectiveness in real-world scenarios.

8. Roadmap and Future Development: Inquire about the software provider's roadmap and future development plans. Understand their commitment to innovation, ongoing enhancements, and the incorporation of emerging technologies. Assess their ability to adapt to evolving industry trends, customer needs, and changing document management requirements. A provider with a forward-thinking approach and a vision for the future can ensure the longevity and relevance of the IDP solution.

By evaluating IDP software providers based on these key factors, you can make a well-informed decision that aligns with your organization's specific needs, maximizes the benefits of automation, and supports your document management journey effectively.

Chapter 6: Implementing IDP: Best Practices

Overview: Implementing Intelligent Document Processing (IDP) requires careful planning, execution, and adherence to best practices to ensure a successful and efficient implementation. In this chapter, we will explore the best practices for implementing IDP, covering various aspects such as project planning, data preparation, system integration, user training, and ongoing optimization. Following these best practices will help you navigate the implementation process smoothly and maximize the benefits of IDP in your document management processes.

1. Project Planning and Scope Definition: Start by defining clear project objectives, scope, and success criteria for your IDP implementation. Identify key stakeholders, allocate resources, and establish a project timeline. Conduct a thorough assessment of your document management needs and establish realistic goals to ensure a focused and successful implementation.
2. Data Preparation and Cleansing: Ensure your documents are properly prepared and cleansed before implementing IDP. This includes standardizing document formats, optimizing image quality and resolution, and organizing documents in a structured manner. Cleanse data by removing any unnecessary noise, inconsistencies, or irrelevant information. Proper data preparation ensures accurate and efficient processing by the IDP system.
3. System Integration and Workflow Design: Integrate the IDP solution into your existing systems and workflows to streamline document processing. Design a workflow that defines how documents will flow through the system, including document ingestion, classification, data extraction, validation, and storage. Ensure seamless integration with other software applications to automate processes and enable smooth data exchange.
4. User Training and Change Management: Provide comprehensive training to users involved in the IDP

implementation. Educate them on how to use the IDP solution, understand its capabilities, and perform tasks efficiently. Create training materials, conduct workshops, and provide ongoing support to help users adapt to the new system and embrace the change. Implement change management strategies to address resistance and ensure smooth transition and user adoption.

5. Continuous Testing and Quality Assurance: Implement a rigorous testing and quality assurance process throughout the IDP implementation. Test the system against a variety of document types, layouts, and scenarios to verify accuracy, efficiency, and system performance. Establish validation and quality control mechanisms to ensure data accuracy and identify and rectify any errors or issues promptly.
6. Incremental Deployment and Iterative Improvement: Consider adopting an incremental deployment approach rather than a big-bang implementation. Start with a subset of documents or processes, pilot the IDP solution, gather feedback, and gradually expand the implementation. This iterative approach allows for learning, optimization, and continuous improvement based on real-world usage and feedback.
7. Monitoring and Optimization: Implement monitoring mechanisms to track the performance and effectiveness of the IDP solution. Continuously monitor key performance indicators (KPIs) such as accuracy rates, processing time, and user feedback. Analyze the data to identify areas of improvement and implement necessary optimizations, such as fine-tuning the system parameters, updating training models, or refining document processing workflows.
8. Security and Compliance Considerations: Ensure that the IDP implementation complies with security and privacy regulations. Implement appropriate security measures to protect sensitive data, such as encryption, access controls, and secure storage. Adhere to relevant compliance standards, such as GDPR or HIPAA, to maintain data privacy and ensure legal and regulatory compliance.

9. Collaboration with Vendor and Community: Maintain an active collaboration with the IDP software vendor and engage with the IDP community. Stay updated on software updates, new features, and best practices shared by the vendor. Leverage the community's knowledge and experiences to learn from others, share insights, and stay informed about the evolving IDP landscape.

By following these best practices, you can effectively implement IDP, optimize your document management processes, and reap the benefits of automation, accuracy, and efficiency in handling your documents.

Designing an Effective Workflow

Designing an effective workflow is crucial for the successful implementation of Intelligent Document Processing (IDP). A well-designed workflow ensures streamlined document processing, efficient task allocation, and optimized use of the IDP solution. In this section, we will explore the details of designing an effective workflow for IDP implementation.

1. Understand Document Flow: Start by gaining a thorough understanding of the document flow within your organization. Identify the different types of documents, their sources, and the processes they go through. Determine how documents are received, sorted, classified, reviewed, validated, and stored. This understanding will form the foundation for designing an effective workflow that aligns with your specific document management needs.
2. Identify Process Steps: Break down the document processing into specific process steps. Each step represents an action or task required to move the document through the workflow. Some common process steps in an IDP workflow include document ingestion, document classification, data extraction, data validation, exception handling, and storage. Identify all the necessary process steps based on your organization's requirements and the capabilities of the IDP solution.

3. Define Task Ownership and Roles: Assign clear ownership and roles for each process step. Determine who is responsible for each task and who will perform it. Designate roles such as document reviewers, data validators, system administrators, or exception handlers. Clearly define the responsibilities and authorities of each role to ensure smooth task allocation and accountability within the workflow.
4. Establish Task Dependencies and Sequencing: Determine the dependencies and sequencing of tasks within the workflow. Identify any prerequisites or dependencies between process steps. Some tasks may need to be completed before others can begin. For example, document classification may need to occur before data extraction can take place. Define the logical order of tasks and ensure that they are sequenced appropriately for efficient document processing.
5. Implement Automation: Leverage the automation capabilities of the IDP solution to automate repetitive and rule-based tasks. Identify tasks that can be automated, such as document classification, data extraction, or validation. Automating these tasks not only improves efficiency but also reduces the likelihood of errors or inconsistencies. Define the rules, conditions, and triggers for automation within the workflow.
6. Exception Handling: Develop a clear process for handling exceptions or errors that may occur during document processing. Determine how exceptions will be identified, flagged, and routed for manual review or resolution. Define the roles and responsibilities for handling exceptions and establish protocols for resolving them in a timely manner. Proper exception handling ensures that errors or issues do not disrupt the overall workflow and document processing.
7. Integration with Existing Systems: Ensure seamless integration of the IDP workflow with your existing systems and software applications. Identify touchpoints where data needs to be exchanged or synchronized between the IDP solution and other systems. Determine the integration mechanisms, such as APIs or connectors, to enable data transfer and workflow

coordination. This integration allows for automated data exchange, reduces manual effort, and ensures data consistency across systems.

8. Document Tracking and Reporting: Implement mechanisms to track the progress of documents through the workflow and generate relevant reports. Establish checkpoints or milestones within the workflow to monitor the status of documents. This allows for transparency, accountability, and visibility into the document processing lifecycle. Generate reports and analytics to measure key performance indicators (KPIs), track productivity, and identify areas for optimization or improvement.
9. Continuous Improvement: Regularly review and refine the workflow based on feedback, data analysis, and evolving business requirements. Monitor the performance of the workflow, identify bottlenecks, and gather insights from user feedback. Continuously optimize the workflow to enhance efficiency, accuracy, and user experience. Stay updated on the latest best practices and industry trends to incorporate improvements into your workflow design.

By following these guidelines, you can design an effective workflow that aligns with your organization's document management needs and optimizes the use of the IDP solution. A well-designed workflow streamlines document processing, enhances efficiency, and maximizes the benefits of IDP in your organization.

Ensuring Scalability and Flexibility

Scalability and flexibility are crucial considerations when implementing Intelligent Document Processing (IDP) solutions. Scalability ensures that your IDP system can handle increasing document volumes and growing processing demands, while flexibility allows for adaptability to evolving business needs and changing document management requirements. In this section, we will explore the details of ensuring scalability and flexibility in your IDP implementation.

1. Evaluate Performance and Capacity: Assess the performance and capacity of your IDP solution to ensure scalability. Consider factors such as processing speed, resource utilization, and system response time. Evaluate whether the solution can handle the projected increase in document volumes and processing requirements over time. Scalable IDP solutions can efficiently process large volumes of documents without compromising performance.
2. Distributed Processing: Consider implementing distributed processing capabilities to enhance scalability. Distributed processing involves dividing the document processing tasks among multiple servers or processing nodes, enabling parallel processing and efficient utilization of resources. This approach allows for handling high volumes of documents and distributing the processing workload across multiple machines, resulting in improved performance and scalability.
3. Cloud-based Solutions: Leverage cloud-based IDP solutions to achieve scalability and flexibility. Cloud platforms provide on-demand scalability, allowing you to scale up or down resources based on your current needs. Cloud-based solutions eliminate the need for hardware investments and enable rapid deployment and scalability without the constraints of physical infrastructure. Additionally, cloud solutions offer flexibility in terms of accessibility, as documents can be processed and accessed from anywhere, facilitating remote work and collaboration.
4. API and Integration Capabilities: Ensure that your IDP solution offers robust API (Application Programming Interface) and integration capabilities. APIs enable seamless integration with other systems, software applications, or third-party services. This allows for data exchange, workflow automation, and streamlined document management processes. The ability to integrate with existing systems enhances scalability and flexibility by leveraging the functionalities and data of other applications in conjunction with the IDP solution.
5. Modular Architecture: Opt for an IDP solution with a modular architecture that allows for flexibility and adaptability. A

modular architecture enables the addition or removal of specific modules or functionalities as per your evolving requirements. This flexibility allows you to customize the IDP solution based on your unique document management needs and scale the system by adding new modules or features as your organization grows.

6. Data Model Flexibility: Ensure that the IDP solution provides flexibility in defining and configuring data models. A flexible data model allows you to adapt the system to accommodate changes in document formats, layouts, or data extraction requirements. The ability to customize data models based on specific document types or fields ensures accurate extraction of relevant information and accommodates varying document structures.
7. Ongoing Performance Monitoring and Optimization: Implement monitoring mechanisms to continuously track the performance of your IDP solution. Monitor key performance indicators (KPIs) such as processing speed, accuracy rates, and resource utilization. Analyze the data to identify areas for improvement and optimization. Regularly review and refine system parameters, configurations, or workflows to enhance scalability and adapt to changing requirements.
8. Vendor Support and Upgrades: Choose an IDP solution from a vendor that offers strong support and regular upgrades. A reliable vendor should provide timely support, address any scalability-related issues, and offer upgrades that improve system performance and scalability. Stay updated on the latest releases and enhancements from the vendor to ensure your IDP solution remains scalable and flexible as technology advances.

By ensuring scalability and flexibility in your IDP implementation, you can accommodate increasing document volumes, adapt to changing business needs, and optimize the efficiency of your document management processes. Scalable and flexible IDP solutions allow for seamless growth and ensure that your organization can handle the evolving demands of document processing.

Integrating IDP with Existing Systems

Integrating Intelligent Document Processing (IDP) with your existing systems is crucial for seamless document management and efficient automation. Integration enables data exchange, workflow coordination, and unified document processing across different systems. In this section, we will explore the details of integrating IDP with existing systems to optimize document management processes.

1. Assess Integration Requirements: Start by assessing the integration requirements specific to your organization. Identify the systems and software applications that are currently in use and play a role in your document management processes. This may include document management systems, customer relationship management (CRM) systems, enterprise resource planning (ERP) systems, or other relevant applications. Understand the data exchange needs, workflow dependencies, and the specific integration points with IDP.
2. API-Based Integration: API (Application Programming Interface) is a common method for integrating systems. Check whether your IDP solution provides APIs that allow for seamless integration with other systems. APIs facilitate communication and data transfer between systems, enabling real-time data exchange, triggering actions, and facilitating workflow automation. Work with your IT team or software developers to utilize the IDP APIs effectively and ensure smooth integration.
3. Data Mapping and Transformation: During integration, ensure that the data formats, structures, and semantics are aligned between the IDP solution and the existing systems. Identify the data fields, attributes, and metadata that need to be mapped or transformed between systems. Develop a data mapping strategy that defines how data will be exchanged, translated, or transformed to ensure compatibility and consistency between systems. Consider data validation and cleansing to maintain data integrity and accuracy during the integration process.

4. Workflow Coordination: Coordinate the workflow between the IDP solution and existing systems to achieve seamless document processing. Define the flow of documents and data between systems, ensuring that each system performs its designated tasks while maintaining the integrity of the overall workflow. Establish triggers, notifications, or event-driven mechanisms to facilitate workflow coordination and ensure that actions in one system initiate the necessary actions in other integrated systems.
5. Synchronization and Data Consistency: Ensure data synchronization and consistency across integrated systems. Establish mechanisms to synchronize data between the IDP solution and other systems to maintain accurate and up-to-date information. Implement strategies such as real-time data updates, batch processing, or scheduled data synchronization to align the data across systems. Data consistency is crucial to avoid discrepancies or errors during document processing and retrieval.
6. Error Handling and Exception Management: Implement error handling and exception management mechanisms to address integration-related issues. Define protocols to handle data transfer failures, system errors, or exceptions that may occur during integration. Establish processes for logging and reporting errors, notifying the appropriate stakeholders, and taking corrective actions. Proper error handling ensures the integrity of document processing and minimizes disruptions in the overall workflow.
7. Security and Access Control: Ensure that security measures are in place to protect data during integration. Implement appropriate access controls, user authentication mechanisms, and data encryption methods to safeguard sensitive information. Establish secure connections and protocols for data transmission between systems. Adhere to industry best practices and compliance regulations to maintain data privacy and ensure secure integration.

8. Testing and Validation: Thoroughly test and validate the integration between the IDP solution and existing systems. Conduct integration testing to verify the seamless exchange of data, synchronization, and workflow coordination. Validate the integrity, accuracy, and consistency of data across systems. Test different scenarios, error conditions, and exception handling processes to ensure that the integration functions as expected in various scenarios.

By effectively integrating IDP with your existing systems, you can streamline document management processes, optimize data exchange, and leverage the capabilities of both the IDP solution and the integrated systems. Integration ensures a cohesive and efficient workflow, reduces manual effort, and enhances the overall document processing experience.

CHAPTER 7: TRAINING AND TESTING IDP MODELS

Overview: Training and testing Intelligent Document Processing (IDP) models are crucial steps in ensuring accurate and reliable document processing and data extraction. In this chapter, we will delve into the details of training and testing IDP models, covering various aspects such as data preparation, model training techniques, evaluation metrics, and iterative improvement. By following best practices in training and testing, you can enhance the performance and effectiveness of your IDP models.

1. Data Preparation: Start by preparing high-quality training data for your IDP models. Gather a diverse and representative dataset that encompasses different document types, layouts, and variations. Cleanse the data by removing noise, inconsistencies, or irrelevant information. Standardize the document formats and ensure proper labeling or annotation of the data to facilitate supervised training. Proper data preparation sets the foundation for accurate and reliable IDP models.
2. Model Selection: Choose the appropriate model architecture and algorithm for your IDP needs. Consider factors such as the complexity of your documents, the type of data to be extracted, and the available computing resources. Commonly used models in IDP include Convolutional Neural Networks (CNNs), Recurrent Neural Networks (RNNs), or Transformer-based models. Select a model that is well-suited to your specific document processing requirements.
3. Supervised Training: Train your IDP models using supervised learning techniques. This involves providing labeled training data, where the input documents are paired with the desired outputs or annotations. Implement techniques such as backpropagation and gradient descent to iteratively update the model's parameters and optimize its performance. Continuously monitor the training process, analyze training curves, and fine-

tune the model as needed to achieve better accuracy and convergence.

4. Evaluation Metrics: Define appropriate evaluation metrics to assess the performance of your IDP models. Common metrics for IDP include accuracy, precision, recall, F1 score, or mean average precision (mAP). Evaluate the model's performance on a held-out validation dataset to measure its accuracy, robustness, and generalization capabilities. Use evaluation metrics to identify areas for improvement and guide model optimization efforts.
5. Test Dataset: Create a separate test dataset to evaluate the final performance of your IDP models. The test dataset should be representative of real-world data that the model will encounter during production use. Evaluate the model's performance on this dataset to obtain an unbiased assessment of its accuracy, reliability, and generalization abilities. Use the test results to determine if the model meets your predefined success criteria and to identify any remaining challenges or areas for improvement.
6. Iterative Improvement: Adopt an iterative approach to continuously improve your IDP models. Analyze the model's performance on the test dataset, identify specific errors or challenges, and update the model accordingly. This may involve additional data collection, refinement of labeling or annotation, architecture modifications, or hyperparameter tuning. Iterate the training and testing process to incrementally enhance the model's accuracy, efficiency, and adaptability to different document types and variations.
7. Transfer Learning and Pretrained Models: Consider leveraging transfer learning and pretrained models to expedite the training process and improve model performance. Transfer learning involves utilizing pretrained models trained on large-scale datasets for related tasks, such as image recognition or natural language processing. Fine-tune these models using your labeled data and specific IDP requirements. Transfer learning can

reduce the need for extensive training data and accelerate the model convergence.

8. Model Versioning and Management: Implement a robust model versioning and management system. Maintain a record of the trained models, including their architectures, parameters, and training configurations. Proper versioning allows for easy tracking of model performance over time and facilitates reproducibility. Additionally, consider implementing model monitoring mechanisms to continuously evaluate the model's performance in real-world scenarios and trigger retraining or model updates when needed.

By following best practices in training and testing IDP models, you can ensure the accuracy, reliability, and efficiency of your document processing and data extraction workflows. Regular evaluation, iterative improvement, and the incorporation of industry advancements will contribute to the ongoing optimization of your IDP models.

Creating a Document Training Set

Creating a high-quality training set is a crucial step in training accurate and reliable Intelligent Document Processing (IDP) models. The training set forms the foundation for the model to learn and generalize patterns from the data. In this section, we will explore the details of creating a document training set for IDP.

1. Data Collection: Start by collecting a diverse and representative dataset of documents that align with your document management needs. Consider the different types of documents and variations you expect the IDP model to encounter during real-world document processing. Gather documents in various formats, such as scanned images, PDFs, or digital documents, to cover a wide range of scenarios.
2. Data Annotation and Labeling: Annotate and label the training data to provide the ground truth for the model during training. Annotation involves identifying and marking the regions of interest within the document, such as fields, tables, or other relevant information. Labeling involves assigning the correct category, tag, or value to each annotated region. Annotating the data accurately and consistently is crucial for training models to learn the desired document structure and information extraction.
3. Manual Annotation vs. Crowdsourcing: Decide whether to perform manual annotation in-house or leverage crowdsourcing platforms. Manual annotation provides control over the quality and consistency of annotations but requires dedicated resources. Crowdsourcing platforms can provide cost-effective solutions for large-scale annotation tasks but require proper guidelines, quality control mechanisms, and validation processes to ensure accuracy and reliability. Choose the approach that best suits your requirements and resources.
4. Data Augmentation: Consider augmenting your training set to enhance its diversity and generalization capabilities. Data augmentation involves introducing variations to the training

data by applying transformations such as rotation, scaling, noise addition, or distortion. Augmentation helps the model learn robust features and improve its ability to handle variations in document formats, layouts, or image quality. However, ensure that the augmented data reflects realistic variations to maintain the relevance of the training set.

5. Data Balance and Distribution: Ensure that your training set is balanced and representative of the real-world distribution of documents. Pay attention to the distribution of different document types, classes, or categories within the training set. A balanced training set prevents bias towards specific document types and ensures that the model learns from a diverse range of samples. If certain classes are underrepresented, consider oversampling or undersampling techniques to address the imbalance.
6. Validation and Quality Control: Implement validation and quality control measures to ensure the accuracy and reliability of the training set. Validate the annotations by comparing them against ground truth or expert annotations. Set up a validation process to review a subset of the annotations and identify and rectify any inconsistencies or errors. Quality control mechanisms help maintain the integrity of the training set and ensure that the model learns from accurate and reliable data.
7. Training Set Size: Consider the size of the training set based on the complexity of the document processing task and the model architecture. Larger training sets can potentially improve the model's performance and generalization ability. However, collecting and annotating a large dataset may not always be feasible. Balance the size of the training set with the available resources and aim for a sufficient sample size that captures the necessary document variations and ensures effective model training.
8. Continuous Expansion and Improvement: Recognize that creating a training set is an ongoing process. As your document management needs evolve, new document types emerge, or variations are encountered, expand and update the training set

accordingly. Continuously gather new data, annotate additional samples, and incorporate them into the training set to improve the model's adaptability to new scenarios and maintain its accuracy and performance over time.

Creating a high-quality training set lays the foundation for training accurate and reliable IDP models. By following these guidelines, you can ensure that your training set is diverse, representative, accurately annotated, and supports effective model training and generalization for your specific document management requirements.

Implementing Supervised Learning Techniques

Implementing supervised learning techniques is a key aspect of training accurate and reliable Intelligent Document Processing (IDP) models. Supervised learning involves training the models on labeled data, where inputs and desired outputs are provided. In this section, we will explore the details of implementing supervised learning techniques for IDP.

1. Data Preparation: Start by preparing the labeled training data for the supervised learning process. Ensure that the data is properly cleaned, standardized, and annotated with accurate labels or ground truth. Remove any irrelevant information or noise from the training data to maintain data quality. Organize the data in a format that is suitable for the training algorithm and the specific requirements of your IDP model.
2. Model Selection: Choose the appropriate model architecture and algorithm for your IDP task. Consider the nature of your documents, the type of data to be extracted, and the available computing resources. Commonly used models in IDP include Convolutional Neural Networks (CNNs), Recurrent Neural Networks (RNNs), or Transformer-based models. Select a model that is well-suited to the structure and characteristics of your document types and the specific information extraction needs.
3. Feature Extraction: Extract relevant features from the input data to feed into the model. Features can be extracted from different modalities, such as text, images, or a combination of both. For text-based features, techniques like word embeddings, bag-of-words, or term frequency-inverse document frequency (TF-IDF) can be used. For image-based features, methods like convolutional layers or pre-trained image recognition models can be employed. Extracting informative features is crucial for the model to learn meaningful patterns and correlations.
4. Model Training: Train the IDP model using the prepared training data and the chosen model architecture. Feed the input

data and the corresponding labels into the model and use an appropriate training algorithm, such as backpropagation with gradient descent, to optimize the model's parameters. During training, the model learns to generalize from the labeled examples and infer the correct information extraction from unseen data. Monitor the training process, analyze training curves, and fine-tune the model as needed to achieve better accuracy and convergence.

5. Hyperparameter Tuning: Perform hyperparameter tuning to optimize the performance of the IDP model. Hyperparameters are the configuration settings of the model that are not learned during training, such as learning rate, batch size, number of layers, or activation functions. Conduct experiments with different hyperparameter values and evaluate their impact on the model's performance. Utilize techniques like grid search, random search, or Bayesian optimization to find the optimal combination of hyperparameters that yield the best results.
6. Cross-Validation: Use cross-validation techniques to assess the model's performance and generalization ability. Split the labeled training data into multiple subsets or folds and perform training and evaluation on different combinations of these folds. This helps estimate the model's performance on unseen data and mitigate issues such as overfitting or bias. Evaluate the model's accuracy, precision, recall, or other relevant metrics using cross-validation to ensure its robustness and reliability.
7. Regularization Techniques: Apply regularization techniques to prevent overfitting and improve generalization. Regularization methods, such as L1 or L2 regularization, dropout, or early stopping, help control the complexity of the model and prevent it from memorizing the training data. Regularization techniques introduce constraints or penalties that encourage the model to learn more generalizable patterns rather than memorizing specific examples.
8. Model Evaluation and Validation: Evaluate the performance of the trained model using a separate validation dataset or through cross-validation. Measure various metrics, such as accuracy,

precision, recall, F1 score, or area under the receiver operating characteristic (ROC) curve, depending on the specific IDP task. Validate the model's ability to correctly extract information from new and unseen documents. Regularly assess the model's performance, iterate on the training process, and implement refinements, as necessary.

By implementing supervised learning techniques effectively, you can train IDP models that accurately extract information from documents and enhance the efficiency of your document processing workflows. Proper data preparation, model selection, feature extraction, and training optimization contribute to the creation of reliable IDP models that generalize well and perform accurately in real-world scenarios.

Conducting Continuous Model Testing and Improvement

Continuous model testing and improvement are essential for maintaining and enhancing the performance of Intelligent Document Processing (IDP) models over time. Regular evaluation, testing, and iterative refinement are crucial to ensure accurate document processing and adaptability to evolving document management needs. In this section, we will explore the details of conducting continuous model testing and improvement for IDP.

1. Test Data Collection: Collect a diverse and representative test dataset that reflects real-world document scenarios. The test dataset should cover various document types, layouts, and variations that the IDP model is likely to encounter during production use. Ensure that the test data is separate from the training and validation data to provide an unbiased evaluation of the model's performance.
2. Evaluation Metrics: Define appropriate evaluation metrics to assess the model's performance. Common evaluation metrics for IDP include accuracy, precision, recall, F1 score, or mean average precision (mAP). Choose metrics that align with your specific document management goals and requirements. These metrics will serve as benchmarks to measure the model's performance during testing and improvement stages.

3. Test Execution: Execute the IDP model on the test dataset to evaluate its performance. Measure and record the model's outputs and compare them with the ground truth or expert annotations. Calculate the evaluation metrics to assess how well the model performs on the unseen data. Analyze the results to identify any areas where the model may be struggling or where performance can be enhanced.
4. Error Analysis: Perform a detailed error analysis to gain insights into the model's weaknesses and areas for improvement. Identify the types of errors made by the model, such as misclassifications, inaccurate extractions, or false positives/negatives. Analyze the patterns and characteristics of these errors to understand the underlying causes. This analysis will guide the improvement process by highlighting the specific aspects of the model that require attention.
5. Iterative Refinement: Iteratively refine the IDP model based on the insights gained from the error analysis. Make targeted adjustments to the model architecture, training data, feature engineering, or hyperparameters to address the identified issues. Modify the training process, introduce new training samples, or adjust the model's configuration to improve its performance on the identified challenges. Repeat the training and testing cycles to assess the impact of the refinements.
6. Data Augmentation and Expansion: Consider augmenting the training data or expanding the dataset to improve the model's performance. Augmentation techniques, such as introducing variations, adding noise, or applying transformations, can help the model learn robust features and generalize better to unseen data. Additionally, continuously gather new data, annotate additional samples, and incorporate them into the training set to improve the model's adaptability and accuracy.
7. Monitoring and Model Versioning: Implement monitoring mechanisms to continuously assess the performance of the IDP model in real-world scenarios. Monitor key performance indicators (KPIs) such as accuracy, recall, or processing time to detect any degradation in performance. Implement a model

versioning system to keep track of different iterations or versions of the model, facilitating comparisons and allowing for rollbacks if necessary.

8. User Feedback and Validation: Leverage user feedback and validation to validate the model's performance and gather insights for improvement. Engage with users who interact with the IDP system and gather their feedback on the accuracy and usefulness of the extracted information. Use this feedback to identify potential issues, validate the model's performance in specific use cases, and prioritize improvement efforts.

By conducting continuous model testing and improvement, you can ensure that your IDP models remain accurate, reliable, and adaptable to evolving document management needs. Regular evaluation, error analysis, iterative refinement, and feedback integration contribute to the optimization of the models' performance over time, leading to more efficient and accurate document processing workflows.

CHAPTER 8: ENSURING DATA SECURITY AND PRIVACY

Overview: Ensuring data security and privacy is of utmost importance when implementing Intelligent Document Processing (IDP) solutions. IDP involves handling sensitive and confidential information, and it is essential to safeguard data throughout its lifecycle. In this chapter, we will explore various aspects of data security and privacy in IDP, including data encryption, access controls, compliance considerations, and risk management. By implementing robust security measures, you can protect your data and maintain the trust of stakeholders.

1. Data Encryption: Implement data encryption techniques to protect sensitive information. Encrypt data both at rest and in transit to prevent unauthorized access. Use strong encryption algorithms and secure key management practices. Encryption ensures that even if data is intercepted or compromised, it remains unreadable and inaccessible to unauthorized individuals.
2. Access Controls: Implement granular access controls to limit access to sensitive data. Define user roles and permissions based on the principle of least privilege. Grant access rights only to authorized individuals who require access for their specific responsibilities. Implement multi-factor authentication (MFA) to strengthen user authentication and prevent unauthorized access.
3. Secure Data Storage: Ensure secure storage of data within the IDP system. Store data in encrypted databases or secure file systems. Implement mechanisms to detect and protect against data breaches, such as intrusion detection systems or security information and event management (SIEM) tools. Regularly update and patch software components to address security vulnerabilities and maintain a secure environment.

4. Compliance Considerations: Adhere to applicable regulations and compliance standards to protect data privacy and maintain legal and regulatory compliance. Consider regulations such as the General Data Protection Regulation (GDPR) or the Health Insurance Portability and Accountability Act (HIPAA), depending on the nature of the data being processed. Implement necessary controls and processes to ensure compliance with these standards.
5. Data Minimization: Adopt a data minimization approach to reduce the amount of sensitive data stored and processed within the IDP system. Minimize the collection and retention of unnecessary or excessive data. Retain data only for as long as necessary to fulfill its intended purpose. By minimizing data, you reduce the potential impact in case of a security breach and enhance data privacy.
6. Risk Management: Implement a comprehensive risk management framework to identify, assess, and mitigate potential risks related to data security and privacy. Conduct risk assessments to identify vulnerabilities and potential threats. Develop risk mitigation strategies, such as implementing security controls, conducting regular security audits, or establishing incident response plans. Continuously monitor and evaluate the effectiveness of risk mitigation measures.
7. Employee Awareness and Training: Ensure that employees are educated and trained on data security and privacy best practices. Raise awareness about potential risks, phishing attacks, or social engineering techniques. Train employees on secure data handling, password management, and the importance of adhering to security policies and procedures. Foster a culture of security awareness and encourage employees to report any suspicious activities promptly.
8. Third-Party Security: Evaluate the security practices of third-party vendors or service providers involved in the IDP implementation. Ensure that they follow robust security measures and comply with relevant standards. Implement contractual agreements that define security obligations and

responsibilities. Regularly monitor and assess the security posture of third parties to maintain the integrity and confidentiality of data.

By implementing robust data security and privacy measures, you can protect sensitive information, maintain regulatory compliance, and mitigate the risks associated with IDP implementations. Safeguarding data throughout its lifecycle builds trust with stakeholders and ensures the integrity of your document management processes.

Implementing Data Encryption and Access Controls

Implementing robust data encryption and access controls is crucial for ensuring data security in Intelligent Document Processing (IDP) implementations. Encryption protects sensitive information from unauthorized access, while access controls ensure that only authorized individuals can access and manipulate the data. In this section, we will explore the details of implementing data encryption and access controls in IDP.

1. Data Encryption:

a. Encryption at Rest: Encrypt data when it is stored or at rest. This involves encrypting files, databases, or storage systems that hold sensitive data. Utilize strong encryption algorithms such as Advanced Encryption Standard (AES) or Triple Data Encryption Standard (3DES). Apply encryption to both structured and unstructured data to maintain its confidentiality and integrity.

b. Encryption in Transit: Encrypt data when it is being transmitted between systems or over networks. Use secure communication protocols such as Transport Layer Security (TLS) or Secure Socket Layer (SSL) to establish encrypted connections. Encrypting data in transit prevents unauthorized interception or eavesdropping on the communication channels.

c. Key Management: Implement secure key management practices to ensure the confidentiality and integrity of encryption keys. Protect encryption keys with strong access controls, such as multi-factor authentication and role-based access controls. Consider using key management systems or

Hardware Security Modules (HSMs) to securely store and manage encryption keys.

d. Tokenization and Obfuscation: Consider employing tokenization or obfuscation techniques for additional data protection. Tokenization replaces sensitive data with non-sensitive substitutes, while obfuscation techniques transform data into a less recognizable or understandable format. These techniques can further enhance data protection while still enabling necessary processing or analytics.

2. Access Controls:

a. User Authentication: Implement strong user authentication mechanisms to verify the identity of individuals accessing the IDP system. Require usernames and passwords with complexity requirements, and encourage the use of multi-factor authentication (MFA) for enhanced security. MFA combines multiple authentication factors, such as passwords, biometrics, or hardware tokens, to provide an additional layer of authentication.

b. Role-Based Access Control (RBAC): Implement RBAC to grant appropriate access privileges based on user roles and responsibilities. Define different roles with specific permissions and access rights. Regularly review and update user roles to ensure that access privileges are aligned with individuals' job functions and responsibilities.

c. Least Privilege Principle: Apply the principle of least privilege, granting users the minimum necessary access rights required to perform their tasks. Restrict access to sensitive data or system functionalities to only those who need them. Regularly review access permissions and revoke unnecessary privileges to minimize the risk of unauthorized access.

d. Audit Trails and Logging: Implement audit trails and logging mechanisms to track user activities and monitor access to sensitive data. Log user actions, data modifications, and system events to detect and investigate any suspicious activities. Regularly review and analyze audit logs to identify potential security incidents or unauthorized access attempts.

e. Data Segregation: Employ data segregation techniques to compartmentalize data based on sensitivity or access requirements. Segment data based on user roles, departments, or other relevant criteria.

Implement logical or physical separation to restrict access to specific data sets and prevent unauthorized access to sensitive information.

f. Regular Access Reviews: Conduct regular access reviews to ensure that access controls remain appropriate and up to date. Periodically review user permissions and access rights to identify any discrepancies or potential security vulnerabilities. Remove access privileges for inactive or terminated users promptly.

g. Encryption of Access Credentials: Encrypt access credentials, such as passwords or authentication tokens, to protect them from unauthorized access. Store encrypted credentials rather than plaintext passwords to enhance security. Utilize strong encryption algorithms and proper key management practices to safeguard access credentials.

By implementing robust data encryption and access controls, you can protect sensitive information, maintain data confidentiality, and minimize the risk of unauthorized access or data breaches. These measures help ensure the integrity of your IDP system and maintain the trust of stakeholders. Regularly review and update your security measures to align with evolving threats and best practices in data security.

Complying with Data Protection Regulations (e.g., GDPR)

Compliance with data protection regulations is essential when implementing Intelligent Document Processing (IDP) solutions, especially with regulations like the General Data Protection Regulation (GDPR). GDPR sets forth guidelines for the collection, processing, storage, and transfer of personal data. In this section, we will explore the details of complying with data protection regulations, focusing on GDPR as an example.

1. Understand Applicable Regulations: Familiarize yourself with the specific data protection regulations that are applicable to your organization, such as GDPR. Study the requirements and guidelines outlined in the regulations to gain a comprehensive understanding of your obligations and responsibilities regarding the handling of personal data.

2. Data Protection Officer (DPO): Appoint a Data Protection Officer (DPO) within your organization, if required by the regulations. The DPO is responsible for ensuring compliance with data protection regulations, providing guidance, and serving as a point of contact for data protection-related matters. The DPO should have expertise in data protection laws and practices.
3. Lawful Basis for Processing: Ensure that you have a lawful basis for processing personal data under the regulations. Identify the appropriate legal basis for processing, such as consent, contractual necessity, legal obligation, vital interests, public task, or legitimate interests. Document the lawful basis and ensure it is communicated to individuals whose data is being processed.
4. Data Subject Rights: Respect and uphold the rights of data subjects as outlined in the regulations. These rights include the right to access, rectify, erase, restrict processing, data portability, and object to processing. Establish processes and procedures to handle data subject requests and provide timely and transparent responses.
5. Privacy Notices: Create and maintain privacy notices that inform data subjects about how their personal data is being processed. The notices should include details such as the purpose of processing, the lawful basis, data retention periods, data recipients, and information about data subject rights. Ensure that privacy notices are easily accessible and written in clear, concise, and understandable language.
6. Data Breach Management: Implement processes and procedures to detect, assess, and manage data breaches in compliance with the regulations. Establish mechanisms for promptly reporting data breaches to the appropriate authorities and, when necessary, to affected individuals. Maintain a record of data breaches and undertake necessary remedial actions to mitigate any adverse effects.
7. Data Transfer Mechanisms: If you transfer personal data outside the jurisdiction covered by the regulations, ensure that

appropriate data transfer mechanisms are in place. Implement mechanisms such as Standard Contractual Clauses (SCCs), Binding Corporate Rules (BCRs), or rely on approved certification mechanisms or codes of conduct. These mechanisms provide adequate safeguards for the protection of personal data during cross-border transfers.

8. Data Protection Impact Assessments (DPIAs): Conduct Data Protection Impact Assessments (DPIAs) for high-risk processing activities, as required by the regulations. DPIAs help identify and mitigate risks to data subjects' rights and freedoms. Assess the necessity and proportionality of the processing, evaluate potential risks, and implement appropriate measures to address those risks.
9. Vendor Management: Implement proper data protection measures when working with third-party vendors or service providers. Ensure that vendors comply with the applicable data protection regulations and implement appropriate data protection safeguards. Establish contractual agreements that clearly outline the responsibilities and obligations of both parties regarding data protection.
10. Data Retention and Disposal: Establish data retention policies and procedures to retain personal data only for as long as necessary. Define retention periods based on legal requirements, the purpose of processing, and organizational needs. Implement secure data disposal practices, such as data anonymization or secure data destruction, when data is no longer needed.
11. Training and Awareness: Provide training and awareness programs to employees involved in the processing of personal data. Educate employees about their responsibilities, data protection principles, and best practices. Regularly update employees on changes in regulations and reinforce a culture of data protection and privacy within the organization.
12. Documentation and Record-Keeping: Maintain documentation and records demonstrating compliance with the regulations. Document processes, procedures, data flows,

privacy impact assessments, and other relevant information. Keep records of data processing activities, data subject requests, data breaches, and any actions taken to address compliance requirements.

Complying with data protection regulations, such as GDPR, is crucial for maintaining the privacy and rights of individuals whose data is being processed. By understanding the requirements, implementing appropriate measures, and fostering a culture of data protection, you can ensure compliance and build trust with data subjects and regulatory authorities.

Performing Regular Security Audits

Regular security audits are essential for assessing the effectiveness of security controls, identifying vulnerabilities, and ensuring the overall security posture of your Intelligent Document Processing (IDP) system. Security audits help uncover weaknesses, mitigate risks, and maintain compliance with industry standards and best practices. In this section, we will explore the details of performing regular security audits in IDP.

1. Define Audit Scope and Objectives: Clearly define the scope and objectives of the security audit. Determine which aspects of the IDP system will be evaluated, such as network security, access controls, data storage, or compliance with specific regulations. Establish specific goals and criteria for the audit, ensuring alignment with organizational policies, industry standards, and regulatory requirements.
2. Select an Audit Methodology: Choose an appropriate audit methodology based on the audit scope and objectives. Common methodologies include a checklist-based approach, risk-based assessments, or compliance-focused audits. Determine the level of detail required and consider involving internal or external auditors with expertise in IDP security.
3. Conduct Vulnerability Assessments: Perform vulnerability assessments to identify potential security weaknesses and vulnerabilities in the IDP system. Utilize automated vulnerability scanning tools or manual assessments to identify security gaps, misconfigurations, or outdated software components. Assess both the infrastructure supporting the IDP system and the software components utilized within it.
4. Penetration Testing: Consider conducting penetration testing to evaluate the security of the IDP system by simulating real-world attacks. Engage with experienced penetration testers to identify potential vulnerabilities that could be exploited by attackers. Penetration testing helps uncover weaknesses in the system's

defenses, allowing for remediation before real-world attacks occur.

5. Review Access Controls: Assess the effectiveness of access controls implemented within the IDP system. Evaluate user authentication mechanisms, role-based access controls (RBAC), and permissions granted to users. Ensure that access rights are granted on a need-to-know basis and that access privileges are regularly reviewed and updated. Assess the handling of privileged accounts and monitor for any potential misuse.
6. Data Security Assessment: Evaluate the security measures implemented to protect data within the IDP system. Assess data encryption methods, data storage practices, and secure transmission protocols. Verify that sensitive data is appropriately masked, anonymized, or encrypted when stored or transmitted. Evaluate data backup and disaster recovery procedures to ensure the availability and integrity of data.
7. Review Incident Response Procedures: Assess the effectiveness of incident response procedures in place to detect, respond to, and mitigate security incidents. Evaluate the incident response plan, including roles and responsibilities, communication channels, and escalation processes. Verify that incidents are properly recorded, investigated, and responded to in a timely manner. Conduct tabletop exercises to test the effectiveness of the incident response plan.
8. Compliance Assessment: Evaluate the IDP system's compliance with applicable regulations, industry standards, and internal policies. Review documentation, privacy notices, data protection impact assessments (DPIAs), and records of data subject requests. Ensure that necessary security controls are in place to comply with specific regulations, such as GDPR or HIPAA. Verify that appropriate security awareness and training programs are in effect.
9. Document Findings and Remediation: Document the audit findings, including identified vulnerabilities, weaknesses, and areas for improvement. Prioritize the findings based on risk severity and potential impact. Develop an action plan to address

the identified issues, assigning responsibilities and timelines for remediation. Regularly review the progress of remediation efforts and ensure that necessary security enhancements are implemented.

10. Continuous Improvement: Use the insights gained from the security audit to drive continuous improvement of the IDP system's security. Implement recommendations, best practices, and lessons learned from the audit process. Regularly repeat the security audit process to monitor progress, assess the effectiveness of remediation efforts, and adapt to evolving threats and industry standards.

Performing regular security audits in IDP is crucial for identifying and mitigating security risks, ensuring compliance, and maintaining a robust security posture. By systematically evaluating security controls, vulnerabilities, and compliance with regulations, you can proactively address security concerns and strengthen the overall security of your IDP system.

CHAPTER 9: AUTOMATING DOCUMENT CAPTURE AND DATA EXTRACTION

Overview: Automating document capture and data extraction processes is a key aspect of Intelligent Document Processing (IDP) implementations. By leveraging automation technologies, organizations can streamline document handling, reduce manual effort, and improve data accuracy and efficiency. In this chapter, we will explore various techniques and tools for automating document capture and data extraction, including optical character recognition (OCR), machine learning, and natural language processing. We will also discuss best practices and considerations for successful automation implementation.

1. Understanding Document Capture: Document capture involves capturing and digitizing documents in various formats, such as scanned images, PDFs, or electronic files. Automating the document capture process eliminates the need for manual data entry and enables faster processing and retrieval of information. It typically includes steps such as document ingestion, image preprocessing, and conversion to machine-readable formats.
2. Optical Character Recognition (OCR): OCR technology plays a crucial role in automating document capture and data extraction. OCR converts scanned images or printed text into machine-readable text. Modern OCR tools utilize advanced algorithms to accurately recognize characters and extract text from images, enabling the automated processing of documents. Implementing OCR improves data accuracy, reduces manual effort, and enhances the efficiency of data extraction.
3. Machine Learning for Data Extraction: Machine learning techniques can be applied to automate data extraction from documents. Through training on labeled data, machine learning models learn to recognize and extract specific data elements, such as names, addresses, or invoice numbers. These models

can be trained using supervised learning techniques, enabling them to generalize patterns and extract data accurately from new documents. Machine learning-based data extraction improves efficiency, scalability, and adaptability.

4. Natural Language Processing (NLP): NLP techniques enhance the automation of document capture and data extraction by enabling the understanding and interpretation of natural language text. NLP algorithms can extract meaning, entities, or relationships from unstructured text, such as emails, contracts, or customer feedback. By utilizing NLP, organizations can automate the extraction of valuable insights and information from a wide range of textual documents.
5. Intelligent Data Extraction: Intelligent data extraction combines OCR, machine learning, and NLP techniques to automate the extraction of structured and unstructured data from documents. It enables the identification and extraction of specific data fields, tables, or entities from documents with complex layouts or varying formats. Intelligent data extraction streamlines data capture processes, reduces errors, and accelerates data availability for further processing and analysis.
6. Automation Workflow Design: Designing an effective automation workflow is crucial for successful document capture and data extraction automation. Define the workflow steps, including document ingestion, preprocessing, OCR, data extraction, and validation. Utilize workflow automation tools or platforms to orchestrate the different steps and ensure smooth and efficient execution. Incorporate error handling, exception management, and validation checkpoints within the workflow to maintain data accuracy and quality.
7. Data Validation and Quality Assurance: Implement validation and quality assurance mechanisms to ensure the accuracy and reliability of the extracted data. Validate extracted data against predefined rules, patterns, or reference data to identify any discrepancies or errors. Implement automated or manual quality checks to verify the correctness of the extracted data. Data

validation and quality assurance processes help maintain data accuracy and integrity throughout the automation workflow.

8. Scalability and Performance Optimization: Consider scalability and performance optimization when automating document capture and data extraction. Ensure that the system can handle large document volumes and scale as the organization's needs grow. Optimize the performance of OCR and data extraction algorithms by leveraging techniques such as parallel processing, distributed computing, or hardware acceleration. Regularly monitor system performance and make necessary adjustments to maintain efficiency.
9. Continuous Improvement: Adopt an iterative approach to continuously improve the document capture and data extraction automation processes. Analyze and learn from the outcomes of the automation, identify areas for improvement, and implement enhancements. Incorporate user feedback, monitor accuracy metrics, and fine-tune algorithms or workflow configurations to optimize the automation process over time.

Automating document capture and data extraction processes streamlines document processing, improves data accuracy, and increases operational efficiency. By leveraging OCR, machine learning, and NLP technologies and following best practices in automation workflow design and quality assurance, organizations can achieve significant productivity gains and unlock valuable insights from their document repositories.

Leveraging Intelligent Capture Technologies

Intelligent Capture Technologies play a crucial role in automating document processing, enabling organizations to extract data accurately and efficiently from various types of documents. These technologies leverage advanced algorithms, artificial intelligence, and machine learning to intelligently interpret and extract relevant information. In this section, we will delve into the details of leveraging intelligent capture technologies for document processing.

1. Document Classification: Intelligent Capture Technologies employ machine learning algorithms to classify documents into predefined categories based on their content, layout, or other features. These algorithms learn from labeled training data to accurately classify incoming documents, such as invoices, contracts, or forms. Document classification streamlines document routing and ensures that the appropriate data extraction rules are applied.
2. Data Extraction and Validation: Intelligent Capture Technologies utilize advanced techniques such as OCR, natural language processing, and machine learning to extract data from documents accurately. These technologies can identify and extract specific data fields, tables, or unstructured information from a wide range of document types. The extracted data is validated against predefined rules, patterns, or reference data to ensure accuracy and integrity.
3. Data Verification and Correction: Intelligent Capture Technologies incorporate data verification mechanisms to validate and correct extracted data. These mechanisms can perform data validation against predefined rules, perform consistency checks, or cross-reference data with external sources. If any discrepancies or errors are detected, the technologies can trigger alerts or provide suggestions for manual review and correction.

4. Exception Handling and Learning: Intelligent Capture Technologies are designed to handle exceptions that occur during the document processing workflow. They can identify documents that require manual intervention or expert review due to low confidence in the extracted data. Exception handling mechanisms allow users to validate and correct data, and these interactions can be used to improve the system's learning capabilities and reduce future errors.
5. Integration with Business Systems: Intelligent Capture Technologies offer integration capabilities to seamlessly integrate with existing business systems and workflows. They can integrate with enterprise content management systems, customer relationship management systems, or other line-of-business applications. This integration enables automated data transfer and synchronization between the intelligent capture system and other systems, ensuring smooth data flow and process automation.
6. Continuous Improvement: Intelligent Capture Technologies employ machine learning algorithms that can improve over time through continuous learning and adaptation. As the system processes more documents and receives user feedback, it can learn from corrections and enhance its data extraction accuracy. Regularly monitor the system's performance, collect user feedback, and leverage analytics to identify opportunities for improvement and refine the underlying models and algorithms.
7. Scalability and Performance: Intelligent Capture Technologies should be scalable to handle large volumes of documents efficiently. They can leverage distributed computing architectures, parallel processing, or cloud-based infrastructure to handle increased workloads and ensure optimal performance. Continuous monitoring of system performance and capacity planning are important to maintain the efficiency and scalability of the intelligent capture system.
8. Security and Compliance: When leveraging intelligent capture technologies, it is crucial to consider security and compliance requirements. Implement robust security measures to protect

sensitive data during document processing and storage. Ensure compliance with relevant data protection regulations, such as GDPR or HIPAA, by implementing appropriate data privacy and security controls. Regularly assess the system's security posture and apply necessary updates or patches to address emerging threats.

By leveraging intelligent capture technologies, organizations can automate document processing, streamline data extraction, and enhance accuracy and efficiency. These technologies enable organizations to handle large volumes of documents while ensuring data accuracy and integrity. With continuous learning capabilities, intelligent capture technologies improve over time, providing organizations with increasingly reliable and efficient document processing capabilities.

Extracting Data from Structured and Unstructured Documents

Data extraction from both structured and unstructured documents is a critical aspect of Intelligent Document Processing (IDP). Structured documents have well-defined layouts and organized data fields, while unstructured documents lack a consistent structure and may contain free-flowing text. Extracting data accurately from both types requires different approaches. In this section, we will explore the details of extracting data from structured and unstructured documents.

1. Structured Document Data Extraction: Structured documents, such as forms, invoices, or surveys, have predefined layouts with consistent data fields. Extracting data from structured documents involves the following steps:

a. Template Design: Create document templates that define the structure and data fields of the document. Templates specify the location and characteristics of each data field to be extracted.

b. Optical Character Recognition (OCR): Utilize OCR technology to convert scanned images or PDFs into machine-readable text. OCR accurately recognizes characters and text from the documents.

c. Text Parsing: Parse the extracted text using text processing techniques to locate and extract data fields based on their positions within the document. This can be achieved through rule-based parsing or regular expressions.

d. Data Validation: Validate the extracted data against predefined rules or patterns to ensure accuracy and integrity. Implement data validation mechanisms to detect and handle errors or inconsistencies.

e. Data Transformation: Convert the extracted data into a standardized format suitable for further processing or integration with other systems. This could involve mapping the data fields to a specific data model or exporting the data in a standardized format such as CSV or XML.

2. Unstructured Document Data Extraction: Unstructured documents, such as contracts, emails, or customer feedback, do not follow a predefined structure, making data extraction more challenging. Extracting data from unstructured documents involves the following steps:

a. Text Mining and Natural Language Processing (NLP): Utilize text mining and NLP techniques to process unstructured text and extract meaningful information. These techniques can identify entities, relationships, or sentiment from the text.

b. Named Entity Recognition (NER): Apply NER algorithms to identify and extract specific entities such as names, dates, locations, or product names from the unstructured text. NER algorithms can be trained using supervised machine learning techniques.

c. Sentiment Analysis: Perform sentiment analysis to determine the sentiment or opinion expressed in the text. This can be valuable for analyzing customer feedback or social media data.

d. Information Extraction: Utilize information extraction techniques, such as rule-based or statistical models, to identify and extract relevant information from unstructured text. This could involve extracting key phrases, events, or structured data from the text.

e. Data Validation and Contextual Analysis: Validate the extracted data and perform contextual analysis to ensure accuracy and consistency. Contextual analysis considers the surrounding text or context to validate and enhance the extracted information.

f. Machine Learning and Training: Utilize supervised or unsupervised machine learning techniques to train models that can recognize and extract specific information from unstructured text. Training the models with labeled data helps improve accuracy and performance.

g. Continuous Improvement: Monitor and evaluate the performance of the data extraction algorithms, collect user feedback, and iteratively refine the models. Continuous improvement ensures that the system learns and adapts to new document patterns and variations.

By employing the appropriate techniques and technologies, organizations can effectively extract data from both structured and unstructured documents. Leveraging OCR, text parsing, NLP, machine learning, and continuous improvement, organizations can automate the data extraction process, enhance accuracy, and improve efficiency in document processing workflows.

Validating and Verifying Extracted Data

Validating and verifying the accuracy and integrity of extracted data is a crucial step in the Intelligent Document Processing (IDP) workflow. Ensuring the quality of extracted data helps maintain data integrity, enables reliable decision-making, and reduces the risk of errors or inconsistencies. In this section, we will explore the details of validating and verifying extracted data.

1. Data Validation against Predefined Rules: Validate the extracted data against predefined rules or patterns to ensure its accuracy and integrity. Define validation rules based on expected data formats, ranges, or business-specific requirements. Perform checks such as data type validation, format validation (e.g., email addresses or phone numbers), or range validation to ensure that the extracted data meets the defined criteria.
2. Cross-Referencing and Data Consistency Checks: Cross-reference the extracted data with other data sources or reference data to ensure consistency and accuracy. Compare extracted data fields with existing databases, reference tables, or external systems to verify their correctness. Perform consistency checks to validate relationships between different data fields, ensuring that the extracted data is internally consistent and coherent.
3. Statistical Analysis and Data Profiling: Conduct statistical analysis and data profiling on the extracted data to identify potential anomalies or outliers. Analyze the distribution, frequencies, or patterns of the data to uncover any inconsistencies or unexpected variations. Statistical techniques such as mean, median, standard deviation, or data clustering can assist in identifying potential data quality issues.
4. Addressing Missing or Incomplete Data: Handle missing or incomplete data elements by implementing appropriate strategies. Detect missing data fields and prompt users or data operators to input the missing information manually. Consider using data imputation techniques to estimate missing values

based on patterns or statistical methods. Apply data validation checks to identify incomplete or inconsistent data and trigger manual intervention if necessary.

5. Data Accuracy Sampling and Verification: Perform manual sampling and verification of the extracted data to validate its accuracy. Randomly select a subset of documents or data records and manually verify the extracted information against the original source documents or authoritative data sources. Compare the extracted data with ground truth or expert annotations to ensure accuracy and identify potential errors or discrepancies.
6. Exception Handling and Error Reporting: Implement mechanisms for handling exceptions and errors encountered during the data validation process. Develop error handling workflows that identify data outliers, inconsistencies, or suspicious data patterns. Establish procedures for reporting and resolving data validation errors, ensuring timely resolution and preventing the propagation of inaccurate or faulty data.
7. User Feedback and Manual Review: Leverage user feedback and manual review processes to validate and verify the accuracy of extracted data. Engage data operators, subject matter experts, or end-users to provide feedback on the quality and accuracy of the extracted data. Encourage users to report any discrepancies or inconsistencies they encounter during their interactions with the extracted data.
8. Continuous Learning and Improvement: Implement continuous learning mechanisms to improve the accuracy and quality of the data extraction process. Leverage user feedback, manual interventions, and identified errors to refine and update the data extraction models or algorithms. Incorporate machine learning techniques to train the system with the corrected data, allowing it to learn from past errors and improve accuracy over time.

By validating and verifying the extracted data, organizations can ensure data accuracy, reliability, and integrity. Implementing validation rules, cross-referencing, statistical analysis, manual verification, and continuous learning practices contribute to the overall data quality assurance in IDP workflows. Reliable and accurate data enhances decision-making, improves operational efficiency, and builds trust in the document processing processes.

CHAPTER 10: ENHANCING IDP ACCURACY AND EFFICIENCY

Overview: Enhancing the accuracy and efficiency of Intelligent Document Processing (IDP) is essential for optimizing document processing workflows and achieving reliable data extraction. This chapter focuses on various strategies, techniques, and best practices to improve the accuracy and efficiency of IDP implementations. We will explore methods to enhance data quality, optimize processing speed, and leverage automation technologies effectively.

1. Data Quality Improvement: a. Preprocessing Techniques: Apply preprocessing techniques such as image enhancement, noise reduction, or deskewing to improve the quality of document images before data extraction. This enhances the accuracy of OCR and improves data extraction results.

b. Intelligent Validation: Implement intelligent validation mechanisms to detect and correct errors in the extracted data. Utilize data validation rules, cross-referencing, and statistical analysis to identify inconsistencies or anomalies. Employ techniques such as fuzzy matching or pattern recognition to handle variations in data formats.

c. Continuous Learning: Leverage machine learning algorithms to continuously learn from user feedback, manual interventions, or data validation processes. Incorporate the insights gained from these processes to improve data extraction models and algorithms over time, enhancing accuracy.

2. Efficient Data Extraction: a. Document Preprocessing: Streamline document preprocessing steps by optimizing OCR settings, document layout analysis, and template design. Utilize OCR tools that offer advanced options for document-specific settings and optimize OCR engines for specific languages or font types.

b. Parallel Processing: Implement parallel processing techniques to optimize the extraction of data from multiple documents simultaneously. Distribute the workload across multiple processing units or utilize distributed computing architectures to enhance processing speed and efficiency.

c. Rule-Based Extraction: Combine rule-based extraction techniques with machine learning models to improve extraction efficiency. Utilize rule-based methods to extract data fields with well-defined patterns or formats, while machine learning models handle more complex or unstructured data extraction tasks.

d. Intelligent Prioritization: Implement intelligent prioritization mechanisms to focus resources on critical or time-sensitive document processing tasks. Prioritize documents based on their importance, urgency, or potential impact on business operations. This ensures that essential documents are processed promptly while optimizing resource allocation.

3. Automation and Integration: a. Workflow Automation: Leverage workflow automation tools or platforms to streamline and automate the end-to-end document processing workflow. Automate document ingestion, data extraction, validation, and integration with downstream systems to eliminate manual tasks, reduce errors, and improve efficiency.

b. Integration with Business Systems: Integrate the IDP solution with existing business systems, such as enterprise content management systems, customer relationship management systems, or ERP systems. Enable seamless data transfer and synchronization between the IDP system and other systems, eliminating manual data entry and ensuring data consistency across applications.

c. API Integration: Utilize APIs (Application Programming Interfaces) provided by IDP solution vendors to integrate the IDP system with other applications or custom workflows. This allows for seamless data exchange, triggering document processing tasks, or accessing extracted data programmatically.

4. Performance Monitoring and Optimization: a. Performance Metrics: Define and monitor performance metrics to measure the accuracy and efficiency of the IDP system. Track metrics such as data extraction accuracy, processing speed, document throughput, or error rates. Regularly analyze these metrics to identify bottlenecks, inefficiencies, or areas for improvement.

b. Continuous Performance Optimization: Continuously optimize the IDP system's performance based on performance metrics and user feedback. Identify areas where performance can be improved, such as optimizing OCR settings, refining extraction models, or enhancing system configurations. Regularly update software components and leverage the latest advancements in IDP technologies.

c. Scalability Planning: Anticipate future growth and document processing demands when designing the IDP system. Implement scalable architectures, utilize cloud-based infrastructure, or employ elastic computing resources to accommodate increasing workloads. Perform capacity planning to ensure the system can scale seamlessly and handle higher volumes of documents.

By focusing on enhancing accuracy and efficiency in IDP, organizations can achieve significant productivity gains, improve data quality, and optimize document processing workflows. Implementing data quality improvement techniques, efficient extraction methods, automation, and performance monitoring enables organizations to achieve accurate and efficient document processing while maintaining scalability and adaptability to evolving needs.

Implementing Document Version Control

Document version control is a critical aspect of document management and Intelligent Document Processing (IDP). It involves maintaining and tracking different versions of documents to ensure accuracy, manage changes, and facilitate collaboration. Implementing document version control processes and tools helps organizations maintain a clear audit trail, enhance collaboration, and avoid confusion caused by multiple versions. In this section, we will explore the details of implementing document version control effectively.

1. Document Naming Conventions: Establish consistent and standardized naming conventions for documents to easily identify and differentiate between different versions. Include version numbers or identifiers in the document filenames or titles to indicate their respective versions. This allows users to quickly identify the most recent version and track document changes.
2. Version Tracking: Utilize a version tracking system or document management software that enables easy tracking and management of document versions. Such systems can automatically assign version numbers or timestamps to documents, making it convenient to identify the latest version. Implement features like version history, revision notes, or change tracking to keep a record of document modifications.
3. Centralized Document Repository: Maintain a centralized document repository or a document management system to store and manage all versions of documents. A centralized repository ensures that authorized users can access the latest version of a document while maintaining version control and avoiding duplication or loss of files. Ensure proper access controls and permissions to manage document security and version access.
4. Check-In/Check-Out Mechanism: Implement a check-in/check-out mechanism to control document access during editing or collaboration. When a user checks out a document for editing, it

becomes temporarily locked to prevent simultaneous conflicting changes. Other users can view the document but cannot edit it until it is checked back in. This mechanism ensures controlled editing and prevents conflicting versions.

5. Version Control Permissions: Define version control permissions and access rights for different user roles or groups. Ensure that only authorized users have the ability to create new versions, modify documents, or control document check-in/check-out. Establish permission levels to restrict access to sensitive or critical documents and prevent unauthorized modifications or deletions.
6. Document Change Management: Establish a change management process to manage document modifications and updates systematically. Clearly define roles and responsibilities for initiating, reviewing, approving, and implementing document changes. Implement workflows or approval mechanisms to ensure proper review and authorization of document modifications before new versions are created.
7. Document Metadata and Annotations: Leverage document metadata and annotations to enhance version control and provide contextual information about document changes. Include relevant information such as the date of the version, author, change description, or comments in the document metadata or annotations. This information helps track and understand the history of document versions.
8. Collaboration and Versioning: Encourage collaborative practices that support version control. Implement collaboration features that allow multiple users to work on a document simultaneously, with changes tracked and merged intelligently. Utilize real-time collaboration tools or version control features in document editing software to ensure smooth collaboration and minimize conflicts.
9. Document Archiving and Retention: Establish document archiving and retention policies to manage document versions effectively. Determine the retention periods for different document versions based on regulatory requirements or business

needs. Archive older versions of documents while retaining access to historical data for reference or compliance purposes.

10. Document Version Auditing: Regularly audit the document version control process to ensure its effectiveness and adherence to organizational policies and regulatory requirements. Perform periodic reviews to verify version accuracy, check compliance with version control processes, and identify areas for improvement.

Implementing effective document version control processes and leveraging appropriate tools facilitates collaboration, maintains document integrity, and ensures accurate tracking of document changes. By implementing standardized naming conventions, utilizing version tracking systems, establishing access controls, and promoting collaboration practices, organizations can efficiently manage document versions and enhance overall document management and IDP workflows.

Utilizing Document Templates and Metadata

Document templates and metadata play a crucial role in streamlining document management processes and improving the efficiency of Intelligent Document Processing (IDP). Templates provide a standardized structure for creating documents, while metadata provides additional information and context about the documents. Leveraging document templates and metadata enables organizations to automate document creation, enhance searchability, and facilitate document classification. In this section, we will explore the details of utilizing document templates and metadata effectively.

1. Document Templates: a. Standardized Document Structure: Document templates provide a predefined structure that ensures consistency and uniformity across documents. They define the layout, formatting, and sections of the document, such as headers, footers, tables, or paragraphs. Standardizing the document structure simplifies data extraction, improves document understanding, and facilitates automated processing.

b. Predefined Data Fields: Document templates can include predefined data fields where specific information needs to be captured. These fields can be placeholders for names, dates, addresses, or other relevant data elements. By utilizing templates with predefined data fields, organizations can automate data extraction processes more accurately and efficiently.

c. Document Classification: Templates aid in document classification by providing indicators of the document type or category. Documents can be categorized based on the template used, allowing for automated routing, processing, and applying specific business rules. This enhances efficiency and ensures that documents are handled appropriately within the IDP system.

d. Version Control: Incorporating version control features within document templates helps manage and track changes across different versions of a document. Templates can be updated, and new versions can be easily identified and managed. This ensures consistency and helps avoid confusion or errors caused by outdated or inconsistent templates.

2. Document Metadata: a. Metadata Definition: Metadata refers to additional information about the document, such as author, date created, keywords, or document classification. Define relevant metadata fields that align with organizational needs and facilitate document retrieval, searchability, and organization. Common metadata fields include title, author, date, document type, or keywords.

b. Automated Metadata Extraction: Implement automated metadata extraction processes to extract relevant metadata from documents automatically. This can be achieved through techniques like OCR, natural language processing, or machine learning algorithms. Automated metadata extraction saves time, improves accuracy, and ensures consistent metadata across documents.

c. Search and Retrieval: Utilize metadata to enhance searchability and retrieval of documents. Tagging documents with descriptive metadata enables users to search and locate documents based on specific criteria or keywords. Users can leverage advanced search functionalities within the IDP system or document management software to find relevant documents quickly.

d. Contextual Information: Metadata provides additional context and insights about the document. It can include information such as document status, associated projects, related entities, or specific data attributes. Contextual metadata facilitates document understanding, aids in decision-making, and enables users to comprehend the document's relevance and importance.

3. Automation and Integration: a. Automated Document Creation: Utilize document templates to automate the creation of new documents. Users can select a relevant template, and the system populates the template with predefined content or placeholders. This streamlines document creation processes, reduces manual effort, and ensures consistency across documents.

b. Integration with Document Management Systems: Integrate the IDP system with a document management system or enterprise content management platform. Link metadata fields from the document management system to the IDP system to ensure consistency and accessibility of metadata across the document lifecycle. This integration facilitates efficient document storage, retrieval, and version control.

c. Workflow Automation: Automate workflows associated with document templates and metadata. Implement rules or triggers that initiate specific actions based on document metadata or template attributes. For example, routing documents for approval based on document type or automatically extracting specific data fields based on metadata properties. Workflow automation improves efficiency and reduces manual intervention.

d. Reporting and Analytics: Leverage metadata for reporting and analytics purposes. Analyze document metadata to gain insights into document usage, trends, or performance metrics. Generate reports on document types, processing times, or user activities to assess system efficiency and identify opportunities for improvement.

By utilizing document templates and metadata effectively, organizations can streamline document creation, enhance searchability and retrieval, improve document classification, and ensure consistency across the document management and IDP workflows. Document templates provide structure and standardization, while metadata adds context and facilitates efficient document organization and retrieval.

Applying Machine Learning for Continuous Improvement

Machine learning plays a significant role in Intelligent Document Processing (IDP) systems by enabling continuous improvement and optimization. By leveraging machine learning algorithms, organizations can enhance the accuracy of data extraction, improve document classification, and automate decision-making processes. In this section, we will explore the details of applying machine learning for continuous improvement in IDP systems.

1. Data Collection and Preparation: a. Collect Labeled Data: Gather a sufficient amount of labeled training data to train machine learning models. Labeled data consists of documents or data samples with annotated ground truth or correct values. This data is used to train models to learn patterns, recognize document types, or extract specific data fields accurately.

b. Data Preprocessing: Preprocess the training data to ensure its quality and prepare it for machine learning algorithms. This may involve removing noise, normalizing data, handling missing values, or balancing the data distribution. Proper data preprocessing improves the learning capabilities of machine learning models.

2. Model Training: a. Select Machine Learning Algorithms: Choose appropriate machine learning algorithms based on the nature of the task, such as classification, regression, or natural language processing. Common algorithms include decision trees, random forests, support vector machines, or deep learning models like convolutional neural networks (CNN) or recurrent neural networks (RNN).

b. Feature Engineering: Perform feature engineering to extract meaningful features from the document data. Features can include text patterns, visual cues, or document layout information. Extracted features help machine learning models understand and generalize patterns in the data, improving accuracy and performance.

c. Model Training and Optimization: Train the machine learning models using the labeled training data. Optimize the models by adjusting hyperparameters, exploring different architectures, or employing techniques like cross-validation or regularization. Model optimization aims to improve generalization, reduce overfitting, and enhance performance on unseen data.

d. Iterative Training: Adopt an iterative training approach, periodically retraining the models with newly labeled or corrected data. As the IDP system processes more documents and collects feedback, incorporate the new data into the training process to continuously improve the accuracy and performance of the models.

3. Model Evaluation and Validation: a. Performance Metrics: Define appropriate performance metrics to evaluate the effectiveness of machine learning models. Metrics can include accuracy, precision, recall, F1 score, or mean average precision (mAP). These metrics provide insights into the models' performance and help identify areas for improvement.

b. Cross-Validation: Utilize cross-validation techniques to assess the models' generalization ability and robustness. Cross-validation involves partitioning the data into training and validation subsets, performing multiple training and evaluation iterations, and averaging the results to obtain more reliable performance estimates.

c. Validation with Ground Truth: Validate the models' performance by comparing the extracted data with ground truth or expert annotations. Assess the accuracy of data extraction, document classification, or any other IDP tasks. Manually validate a representative sample of processed documents to ensure high-quality results.

4. Continuous Learning and Adaptation: a. Feedback Loop: Establish a feedback loop that captures user feedback, manual interventions, or corrections made during the document processing workflow. Incorporate this feedback into the machine learning pipeline to update and refine the models continuously.

b. Model Re-training: Regularly retrain the models with new labeled data, corrected data, or feedback. Incorporate the retraining process into the IDP system's workflow to ensure the models adapt to evolving document patterns, new document types, or changes in data characteristics.

c. Model Versioning: Implement model versioning mechanisms to track and manage different versions of machine learning models. Maintain a history of model versions, allowing for easy rollback or comparison of performance between different versions.

5. Performance Monitoring and Maintenance: a. Performance Monitoring: Continuously monitor the performance of the machine learning models in the live production environment.

Monitor accuracy, data extraction errors, or classification performance to detect any degradation or identify areas that require further improvement.

b. Anomaly Detection: Implement anomaly detection techniques to identify unusual patterns or errors in the document processing results. Detect outliers, inconsistencies, or potential errors by comparing the extracted data against expected patterns or predefined thresholds.

c. Maintenance and Updates: Regularly update the machine learning models, algorithms, or underlying libraries to incorporate the latest advancements and improvements. Stay informed about emerging research and best practices in IDP and machine learning to enhance the system's accuracy, efficiency, and adaptability.

By applying machine learning for continuous improvement, organizations can enhance the accuracy and efficiency of their IDP systems. Through data collection, model training, evaluation, and continuous learning, machine learning models can adapt to evolving document patterns, improve data extraction accuracy, and automate decision-making processes, contributing to ongoing optimization and increased efficiency in document processing workflows.

Chapter 11: Intelligent Document Classification

Overview: Intelligent Document Classification is a crucial component of Intelligent Document Processing (IDP) that involves automatically categorizing documents into predefined classes or categories. It enables organizations to streamline document management, automate workflows, and extract relevant information more effectively. This chapter focuses on the techniques, strategies, and best practices for intelligent document classification.

1. Importance of Document Classification: Document classification brings numerous benefits to organizations, including:

- Efficient Document Organization: Classifying documents into categories allows for efficient organization and retrieval, reducing the time spent searching for specific documents.
- Workflow Automation: Document classification enables the automation of document routing, processing, and assignment based on their categories, improving operational efficiency.
- Data Extraction Accuracy: Classification helps tailor data extraction algorithms to specific document types, enhancing the accuracy of data extraction and reducing errors.
- Compliance and Security: Classification aids in applying appropriate security measures, access controls, and compliance requirements based on document categories.

2. Document Classification Techniques: a. Rule-Based Classification: Rule-based classification involves defining specific rules or patterns to assign documents to predefined classes. Rules may consider keywords, document properties, or specific patterns within the document content or layout.

b. Machine Learning-based Classification: Machine learning algorithms can be trained to automatically learn patterns and features from labeled training data to classify documents. Techniques such as Naive Bayes, Support Vector Machines (SVM), Decision Trees, or Neural Networks are commonly used.

c. Hybrid Approaches: Hybrid approaches combine rule-based and machine learning techniques for document classification. Rules can be used as initial classifiers, and machine learning models can refine the classification based on the learned patterns from training data.

3. Document Feature Extraction: Extracting relevant features from documents is essential for effective classification. Features can include text content, visual cues, document layout, or metadata. Feature extraction techniques depend on document types and may involve text analysis, image processing, or natural language processing (NLP) algorithms.
4. Training Data and Model Development: Developing accurate classification models requires sufficient and diverse training data. Labeled training data represents documents with their respective classes. The training data is used to train machine learning models, adjust parameters, and improve the classification accuracy. Careful data preprocessing, feature selection, and model optimization enhance the performance of the classification models.
5. Model Evaluation and Validation: Evaluate the performance of classification models using appropriate evaluation metrics such as accuracy, precision, recall, or F1-score. Utilize techniques like cross-validation to assess the models' generalization ability. Validate the models using a separate validation dataset or perform manual validation to ensure accuracy and consistency.
6. Continuous Improvement: Continuously improve the classification models by incorporating user feedback and leveraging manual review processes. Monitor model performance, collect feedback on misclassified documents, and

periodically update and retrain the models to adapt to evolving document patterns or new document classes.

7. Integration with Document Workflows: Integrate the intelligent document classification system with document workflows to automate document routing, processing, or assignment. Link document classification results with other IDP modules such as data extraction or document prioritization to streamline the overall document processing workflow.
8. Scalability and Adaptability: Design the document classification system to handle increasing document volumes and accommodate new document types. Ensure the system is scalable, robust, and adaptable to changing business needs. Regularly evaluate the system's performance, optimize computational resources, and consider cloud-based solutions for scalability.

Intelligent document classification simplifies document management, accelerates information retrieval, and enhances data extraction accuracy. By applying the appropriate classification techniques, leveraging machine learning, and continuously improving the models, organizations can optimize document workflows, automate processes, and extract valuable insights from their document repositories.

Categorizing Documents Based on Content and Purpose

Categorizing documents based on their content and purpose is a fundamental aspect of intelligent document classification. By understanding the content and purpose of documents, organizations can effectively organize, retrieve, and process them. This section delves into the details of categorizing documents based on their content and purpose.

1. Content-Based Categorization: Content-based categorization focuses on the actual text, images, or data within a document. It involves analyzing the document's content to determine its category. Some techniques for content-based categorization include:

a. Text Analysis: Analyze the textual content of the document using natural language processing (NLP) techniques. This can involve techniques like keyword extraction, named entity recognition, sentiment analysis, or topic modeling to identify specific features or attributes that define the document's category.

b. Image Processing: Apply image processing techniques to analyze visual content within documents. This can involve optical character recognition (OCR) to extract text from images, image feature extraction to identify visual patterns, or object recognition to classify documents based on specific visual elements.

c. Data Analysis: Analyze structured or semi-structured data within documents, such as spreadsheets or databases. Utilize data mining or data analytics techniques to identify patterns, relationships, or characteristics that determine the document category.

2. Purpose-Based Categorization: Purpose-based categorization focuses on the intended purpose or function of the document. It involves understanding why the document was created and classifying it accordingly. Some techniques for purpose-based categorization include:

a. Document Templates: Utilize predefined document templates to categorize documents based on their intended purpose. Templates provide a structure that reflects the specific purposes of different document types, such as invoices, contracts, reports, or presentations.

b. Metadata Analysis: Leverage metadata associated with documents to categorize them based on their purpose. Metadata can include information like document type, author, creation date, or keywords. Analyzing this metadata provides insights into the purpose of the document and facilitates categorization.

c. Contextual Analysis: Consider the context in which the document is used, or the business processes it is associated with. Analyze the document's role within the organization, its relationship to other documents or systems, or the workflows it supports. This contextual analysis helps determine the purpose and categorization of the document.

3. Hybrid Approaches: Combining content-based and purpose-based categorization techniques often yields more accurate results. Hybrid approaches leverage both the document's content and its intended purpose to classify documents effectively. By combining the strengths of content analysis and purpose analysis, hybrid approaches enhance classification accuracy and provide a comprehensive understanding of the document's categorization.
4. Training Data and Model Development: Developing accurate models for content and purpose-based categorization requires high-quality training data. Collect a diverse set of labeled documents that represent various categories. This data is used to train machine learning models, such as decision trees, support vector machines (SVM), or deep learning models, to learn patterns and make accurate categorization predictions.
5. Continuous Improvement: Continuously improve the categorization models by incorporating user feedback and manual validation. Periodically review and update the models based on new document patterns or emerging categories. Incorporate an iterative feedback loop to ensure the models adapt to evolving document content and purpose.

Categorizing documents based on content and purpose enhances document management, retrieval, and processing. By leveraging content analysis, purpose analysis, or hybrid approaches, organizations can effectively categorize documents, streamline workflows, and automate document processing based on their content and intended purpose.

Implementing Automated Document Routing

Automated document routing is a crucial aspect of Intelligent Document Processing (IDP) that enables organizations to streamline document workflows and ensure documents reach the right recipients or systems efficiently. Implementing automated document routing involves leveraging document attributes, metadata, or content to determine the appropriate recipients or destinations. This section explores the details of implementing automated document routing effectively.

1. Document Attributes and Metadata: Utilize document attributes and metadata to drive automated document routing. These attributes can include document type, sender, recipient, keywords, document creation date, or any other relevant information. By extracting and analyzing these attributes, the routing system can determine the appropriate recipients or destinations for the document.
2. Rule-Based Routing: Implement rule-based routing mechanisms to define routing rules based on specific document attributes or conditions. Rules can be created to match certain keywords, sender details, or document types and then route the document accordingly. For example, if a document contains the keyword "Invoice," it can be automatically routed to the finance department.
3. Intelligent Content Analysis: Leverage intelligent content analysis techniques, such as natural language processing (NLP), to analyze the document content and extract relevant information. NLP can help identify entities, topics, or specific data fields within the document that can guide the routing process. For example, if a document mentions a specific project or customer, it can be routed to the corresponding project team or account manager.
4. Workflow Integration: Integrate the automated document routing system with existing workflows, document management systems, or enterprise content management platforms. Ensure that the routing system seamlessly integrates with other systems to retrieve relevant information, update document statuses, and trigger subsequent workflow actions.
5. User-Based Routing: Incorporate user-based routing to allow individual users or groups to define their preferred routing rules. Users can set up personalized rules or preferences for document routing based on their roles, responsibilities, or specific requirements. This empowers users to customize their document routing and ensures efficient handling of documents within their areas of expertise.

6. Dynamic Routing: Implement dynamic routing mechanisms that dynamically assign recipients or destinations based on real-time conditions or workload. For example, if a specific department or individual is overloaded with documents, the system can dynamically route documents to other available resources to balance the workload and ensure timely processing.
7. Exception Handling: Define rules and mechanisms to handle exceptional cases where automated routing may not be possible or appropriate. Establish fallback options or manual intervention processes to handle documents that cannot be automatically routed. Implement escalation procedures or notifications to ensure prompt handling of exceptional situations.
8. Audit Trails and Monitoring: Maintain audit trails and logs to track the routing history of documents. This provides transparency, accountability, and visibility into the document routing process. Monitor the routing system's performance and effectiveness to identify bottlenecks, refine rules, or optimize the routing process for improved efficiency.
9. Performance Measurement and Optimization: Establish performance metrics to measure the efficiency and accuracy of the automated document routing system. Monitor and analyze key metrics such as routing accuracy, processing time, or document throughput. Utilize these insights to identify areas for improvement, refine routing rules, or optimize the system's performance.
   10. Scalability and Adaptability: Design the automated document routing system to handle increasing document volumes and accommodate changing business needs. Ensure the system is scalable, robust, and adaptable to handle diverse document types, formats, and routing requirements. Regularly evaluate and optimize the system's performance to meet evolving business demands.

Implementing automated document routing streamlines document workflows, reduces manual intervention, and ensures documents are efficiently delivered to the right recipients or systems. By leveraging document attributes, metadata, content analysis, and integrating with existing workflows, organizations can achieve efficient document routing, improve operational efficiency, and enhance overall document processing workflows.

Optimizing Classification Accuracy with Machine Learning

Optimizing classification accuracy is crucial in Intelligent Document Processing (IDP) to ensure precise document categorization and enable reliable downstream processes. Machine learning techniques can significantly enhance classification accuracy by leveraging patterns and features in the data. This section delves into the details of optimizing classification accuracy with machine learning.

1. High-Quality Training Data: High-quality training data is essential for building accurate classification models. Collect a diverse and representative set of labeled training data that covers various document classes and instances. Ensure the training data captures the intricacies and variations present in the documents to improve the model's ability to generalize.
2. Feature Selection and Engineering: Feature selection and engineering aim to extract relevant information from the documents for classification. Identify informative features that discriminate between different document classes. This can involve techniques like term frequency-inverse document frequency (TF-IDF), word embeddings, image features, or other domain-specific features. Experiment with different feature sets to identify the most discriminative features for accurate classification.
3. Algorithm Selection and Optimization: Choose appropriate machine learning algorithms that are suitable for the classification task. Common algorithms include decision trees, random forests, support vector machines (SVM), k-nearest neighbors (k-NN), or deep learning models like convolutional neural networks (CNN) or recurrent neural networks (RNN). Optimize the algorithms by tuning hyperparameters, adjusting

regularization techniques, or exploring ensemble methods to improve classification accuracy.

4. Cross-Validation and Evaluation: Utilize cross-validation techniques to assess the model's performance and generalize its ability to unseen data. Partition the labeled training data into training and validation subsets and perform multiple iterations to evaluate the model's performance across different data samples. Evaluate the model using appropriate evaluation metrics such as accuracy, precision, recall, F1-score, or area under the receiver operating characteristic curve (AUC-ROC).
5. Ensemble Techniques: Ensemble techniques combine multiple classification models to improve accuracy. Ensemble methods, such as bagging, boosting, or stacking, leverage the collective decisions of multiple models to enhance classification performance. By combining the strengths of different models or variations of the same model, ensemble techniques can mitigate individual model biases and improve overall accuracy.
6. Data Augmentation: Data augmentation techniques can help address data scarcity issues and enhance the model's ability to generalize. Augmentation involves generating additional training data by applying transformations or modifications to the existing data. For text data, techniques like word replacement, synonym substitution, or text synthesis can be employed. For image data, techniques like rotation, scaling, or cropping can be used. Augmenting the data increases the diversity of the training set and improves the model's ability to handle variations in the documents.
7. Transfer Learning: Transfer learning leverages pre-trained models on large-scale datasets to enhance classification accuracy. Pre-trained models, such as deep learning models trained on general image or text datasets, can be fine-tuned on the specific document classification task. By utilizing the pre-trained models' learned features and knowledge, transfer learning allows for effective classification with limited training data.

8. Model Iteration and Continuous Learning: Continuously iterate and refine the classification models based on feedback, manual validation, or performance monitoring. Incorporate user feedback or expert knowledge to update the models and improve accuracy. Implement a continuous learning process that re-trains the models periodically with new labeled data or incorporates updates to the classification algorithms.
9. Error Analysis and Model Improvement: Perform error analysis to identify patterns or common misclassifications made by the models. Analyze misclassified documents to understand the reasons behind the errors. Adjust the models, update the feature extraction techniques, or refine the training data based on the insights gained from error analysis. Iteratively improve the models to reduce misclassification rates and enhance accuracy.

Optimizing classification accuracy with machine learning requires a combination of data quality, feature selection, algorithm optimization, and iterative improvement. By leveraging high-quality training data, selecting appropriate algorithms, utilizing ensemble techniques, and incorporating continuous learning, organizations can achieve higher accuracy in document classification, leading to more effective document processing and improved downstream tasks.

CHAPTER 12: EXTRACTING AND VALIDATING DATA FROM DOCUMENTS

Overview: Chapter 12 focuses on the critical process of extracting and validating data from documents in the context of Intelligent Document Processing (IDP). Efficient and accurate data extraction is essential for organizations to automate data-intensive workflows, improve operational efficiency, and enable reliable decision-making. This chapter explores various techniques, strategies, and best practices for extracting and validating data from documents.

1. Importance of Data Extraction: Data extraction involves identifying and capturing relevant information from documents. Accurate data extraction is crucial for several reasons:

- Automation and Efficiency: Extracted data can be utilized to automate manual processes, reducing human effort and improving operational efficiency.
- Data Integration: Extracted data can be integrated with other systems, databases, or analytics platforms, enabling seamless data flow and analysis.
- Decision-Making: Extracted data provides valuable insights for informed decision-making, trend analysis, or predictive modeling.
- Compliance and Audit: Accurate data extraction ensures compliance with regulations, facilitates audits, and supports traceability.

2. Data Extraction Techniques: a. Rule-Based Extraction: Rule-based extraction involves defining specific rules or patterns to identify and extract data fields from documents. These rules can be based on keywords, regular expressions, positional

information, or document structure. Rule-based extraction is suitable for structured or semi-structured documents with consistent layouts.

b. Machine Learning-Based Extraction: Machine learning techniques, such as supervised learning or sequence labeling, can be used for data extraction. Models are trained on labeled data to learn patterns and extract relevant data fields automatically. Machine learning-based extraction is particularly useful for unstructured or semi-structured documents with varying layouts or formats.

c. Optical Character Recognition (OCR): OCR technology converts scanned or image-based documents into editable and searchable text. OCR enables the extraction of textual information from documents that are not machine-readable, such as scanned invoices, receipts, or handwritten forms. The extracted text can then be processed for further data extraction.

3. Data Validation and Quality Assurance: Data validation ensures the accuracy, consistency, and integrity of the extracted data. It involves verifying the extracted data against predefined rules, validation checks, or external data sources. Key aspects of data validation include:

- Format Validation: Validate the extracted data fields to ensure they adhere to the expected formats, such as date formats, numerical values, or specific patterns.
- Data Consistency: Validate the relationships between different data fields to ensure consistency and logical coherence.
- External Data Validation: Validate the extracted data by comparing it against external data sources or reference databases to ensure accuracy and completeness.

4. Confidence Scoring: Assign confidence scores to extracted data fields to quantify the level of confidence or reliability. Confidence scores indicate the certainty of the extracted data and help prioritize manual review or validation efforts. Machine

learning techniques, rule-based approaches, or statistical methods can be employed to assign confidence scores based on factors like extraction accuracy, document quality, or historical performance.

5. Human-in-the-Loop Validation: Incorporate human validation or review processes to validate and verify extracted data fields. Human reviewers manually review a sample of extracted data or handle exceptions that cannot be confidently automated. Human-in-the-loop validation helps refine extraction rules, improve accuracy, and handle complex document scenarios.
6. Continuous Improvement: Implement a feedback loop to collect user feedback, monitor data quality, and identify areas for improvement. Regularly evaluate the performance of the data extraction system, address issues, and refine extraction rules or machine learning models based on user feedback and evolving document patterns.
7. Data Security and Privacy: Implement appropriate security measures to protect the extracted data, ensuring compliance with data privacy regulations. Encryption, access controls, and data anonymization techniques should be implemented to safeguard sensitive information extracted from documents.
8. Integration with Downstream Systems: Ensure seamless integration of the extracted data with downstream systems, databases, or workflow automation tools. Define appropriate data formats, interfaces, or APIs to enable data transfer and processing in other systems or processes.

By implementing effective data extraction and validation techniques, organizations can automate data-intensive processes, improve operational efficiency, and enhance data-driven decision-making. Accurate and validated data extraction empowers organizations to unlock the full potential of their document repositories and extract valuable insights for improved business outcomes.

Identifying Key Data Elements in Documents

Identifying key data elements in documents is a crucial step in Intelligent Document Processing (IDP) that enables organizations to extract and leverage relevant information for automation, analysis, or decision-making. Key data elements represent the critical pieces of information within documents that hold significant value. This section explores the details of identifying key data elements in documents.

1. Document Understanding: To identify key data elements, it is essential to have a thorough understanding of the document's structure, content, and purpose. Analyze the document to determine its layout, sections, headers, footers, and any repeating patterns. Understand the context and meaning of the document to identify the data elements that carry the most relevance and impact.
2. Business Requirements and Use Cases: Consider the specific business requirements and use cases that drive the need for document processing. Identify the information elements within the documents that are vital for fulfilling these requirements. Work closely with stakeholders, subject matter experts, and end-users to determine the critical data elements they need to extract from the documents.
3. Data Field Identification: Scan the document to identify the different data fields or information sections. These can be textual fields, numeric fields, dates, addresses, or any other specific data formats. Determine the labels or names associated with these fields, if available, to aid in their identification.
4. Semantic Analysis: Apply semantic analysis techniques to understand the meaning and context of the document content. This can involve natural language processing (NLP) algorithms, such as part-of-speech tagging, named entity recognition, or relationship extraction. By analyzing the semantic structure of the document, you can identify key data elements that carry important information for the intended use cases.
5. Document Layout Analysis: Analyze the document layout and structure to identify key data elements. Look for consistent patterns, locations, or formatting cues that indicate the presence

of critical information. This may involve identifying data tables, form fields, or specific sections within the document that contain important data.

6. Machine Learning-Based Approaches: Leverage machine learning algorithms, such as information extraction or named entity recognition models, to automatically identify key data elements. Train these models using labeled training data that includes examples of the key data elements you wish to identify. Machine learning models can learn patterns, context, and relationships within the document to accurately identify the relevant data elements.
7. Document-specific Heuristics: Develop document-specific heuristics or rules to identify key data elements based on the document structure, content, or specific characteristics. These rules can be based on document templates, keywords, regular expressions, or positional information. Establishing document-specific rules helps improve accuracy and reliability in identifying the key data elements.
8. Feedback and Iterative Refinement: Incorporate feedback loops and iterative refinement processes to improve the identification of key data elements. Collect user feedback, analyze extraction results, and refine the identification techniques based on the insights gained. Continuously improve the identification process to adapt to evolving document patterns or variations.
9. Human Validation: Include human validation or review processes to validate and verify the identification of key data elements. Human reviewers can manually review and confirm the identified data elements, handling complex or ambiguous cases that require human judgment. Human validation helps refine identification rules, improve accuracy, and handle document-specific nuances.

Identifying key data elements in documents is a crucial step in extracting valuable information and automating document processing workflows. By understanding the document, aligning with business requirements, leveraging machine learning algorithms, and incorporating human validation, organizations can accurately identify the key data elements that are essential for achieving their document processing objectives.

Implementing Data Extraction Techniques (e.g., Named Entity Recognition)

Data extraction techniques, such as Named Entity Recognition (NER), play a vital role in Intelligent Document Processing (IDP) to automatically identify and extract specific information from documents. NER focuses on identifying and categorizing named entities, such as names, locations, dates, organizations, or other domain-specific terms, within the document. This section explores the details of implementing NER and other data extraction techniques.

1. Preparing Training Data: To implement NER, prepare a labeled training dataset that includes examples of the named entities you want to extract. Label the entities within the training data to indicate their specific categories, such as person names, addresses, or product names. The training data should cover a diverse range of examples to ensure the model learns to recognize different variations and contexts.
2. Selecting NER Algorithms: Choose appropriate NER algorithms based on the nature of your documents and the entities you wish to extract. Common algorithms include rule-based approaches, statistical models, or deep learning models. Rule-based approaches rely on predefined patterns or rules to extract entities, while statistical models and deep learning models learn from labeled data to recognize entities based on patterns and context.
3. Training NER Models: Train NER models using the labeled training dataset. This involves feeding the labeled data into the selected NER algorithm to learn the patterns and characteristics of the named entities. The training process aims to optimize the model's ability to recognize and extract entities accurately.
4. Feature Engineering: Perform feature engineering to enhance the NER models' performance. Feature engineering involves selecting or engineering relevant features from the document

data that contribute to the identification of named entities. Features can include word embeddings, part-of-speech tags, syntactic dependencies, or contextual information. Experiment with different features to improve the model's accuracy and generalization.

5. Model Evaluation and Optimization: Evaluate the performance of the NER models using appropriate evaluation metrics, such as precision, recall, or F1-score. Utilize techniques like cross-validation to assess the models' generalization ability. Optimize the models by adjusting hyperparameters, exploring different architectures, or employing techniques like dropout or regularization to improve performance and mitigate overfitting.
6. Integration with Document Processing Workflow: Integrate the NER models into the document processing workflow. Connect the NER models with other IDP components, such as document classification, data validation, or workflow automation systems. Incorporate the NER models into the larger IDP pipeline to extract relevant entities and facilitate downstream processes.
7. Handling Entity Ambiguity and Variations: Consider cases where entities exhibit variations, aliases, or ambiguity. Develop strategies to handle these cases effectively. This can involve expanding the training data to include various forms and variations of entities, leveraging context or surrounding information for disambiguation, or applying entity resolution techniques to resolve potential ambiguities.
8. Continuous Learning and Improvement: Implement a feedback loop to collect user feedback, monitor performance, and continuously improve the NER models. Periodically retrain the models with new labeled data or incorporate user feedback to refine the models' accuracy and adapt them to evolving document patterns or entity variations.
9. Customization and Domain Adaptation: If your documents contain domain-specific named entities, consider customizing or fine-tuning the NER models to improve their performance in your specific domain. Customization involves training the

models on domain-specific data to recognize and extract entities relevant to your domain accurately.

Implementing NER and other data extraction techniques enhances the accuracy and efficiency of document processing workflows. By preparing training data, selecting appropriate algorithms, training models, performing feature engineering, and integrating with the document processing workflow, organizations can effectively extract valuable information from documents and automate data-intensive processes.

Performing Data Validation and Quality Control Checks

Data validation and quality control are crucial steps in Intelligent Document Processing (IDP) to ensure the accuracy, consistency, and integrity of extracted data. By implementing robust validation and quality control checks, organizations can identify and address data errors, inconsistencies, or anomalies, ensuring the reliability of the extracted data. This section explores the details of performing data validation and quality control checks.

1. Define Validation Rules: Establish validation rules based on the expected format, structure, or content of the extracted data. These rules should align with the specific requirements and constraints of the data fields. Validation rules can include data type checks, format checks (e.g., date format), range checks (e.g., numerical values within a specific range), or consistency checks (e.g., verifying relationships between related data fields).
2. Data Consistency Checks: Ensure data consistency by validating relationships and dependencies between different data fields. Perform checks to ensure that the extracted data fields are logically coherent and consistent with each other. For example, if a document contains invoice details, validate that the invoice amount matches the sum of individual line items.
3. External Data Validation: Validate the extracted data against external data sources or reference databases to ensure accuracy and completeness. Compare the extracted data with known values or reference data to verify its validity. This can involve

cross-referencing against external systems, performing lookup operations, or utilizing third-party data providers.

4. Format and Structure Validation: Validate the format and structure of the extracted data fields. Ensure that the data adheres to the expected formats, such as date formats, numerical values, or specific patterns. Validate structured data fields against predefined templates or patterns to ensure conformity.
5. Duplicate and Inconsistent Data Checks: Detect and handle duplicate or inconsistent data entries within the extracted data. Implement checks to identify duplicates or similar entries and apply deduplication techniques. Identify and address inconsistencies in data fields that should have consistent values across documents or data records.
6. Error Handling and Exception Management: Define error handling and exception management processes to handle data validation errors. Establish protocols for handling validation failures, such as generating error reports, flagging erroneous data entries, or triggering manual review processes. Develop escalation procedures to address exceptional cases or data anomalies that cannot be resolved automatically.
7. Confidence Scoring and Confidence Thresholds: Assign confidence scores or probabilities to the extracted data fields to quantify the level of confidence or reliability. Establish confidence thresholds to determine when manual intervention or further review is required. Data fields with low confidence scores can be flagged for manual verification or review to ensure accuracy.
8. Sampling and Manual Validation: Implement sampling techniques to select a subset of extracted data for manual validation. Human reviewers can manually review and validate the accuracy of the extracted data fields. Use the manual validation results to assess the performance of the data extraction system, refine extraction rules, or identify areas for improvement.
9. Continuous Improvement: Implement a feedback loop to collect user feedback, monitor data quality, and drive continuous

improvement. Regularly evaluate the performance of the data extraction and validation processes, address issues, and refine rules or models based on user feedback and evolving document patterns.

10. Audit Trails and Data Governance: Maintain comprehensive audit trails and logs to track the validation process and changes made to the extracted data. Implement data governance practices to ensure data integrity, traceability, and accountability throughout the validation and quality control processes.

By performing data validation and quality control checks, organizations can ensure the accuracy and reliability of the extracted data. By defining validation rules, checking data consistency, validating against external sources, and implementing error handling processes, organizations can improve data quality and enhance the overall reliability of their IDP systems.

CHAPTER 13: INTEGRATING IDP WITH BUSINESS PROCESSES

Overview: Chapter 13 focuses on the critical aspect of integrating Intelligent Document Processing (IDP) with business processes. Integration allows organizations to leverage the power of IDP to streamline and automate document-driven workflows, enhance operational efficiency, and drive digital transformation. This chapter explores various techniques, strategies, and best practices for effectively integrating IDP with business processes.

1. Understanding Business Processes: Before integrating IDP, it is crucial to have a deep understanding of the existing business processes and document workflows within the organization. Analyze how documents are generated, received, processed, and stored throughout the different stages of the business processes. Identify pain points, inefficiencies, or areas where IDP can add the most value.
2. Mapping Document Touchpoints: Map the touchpoints where documents interact with different stages or participants in the business processes. This involves identifying the entry points for documents, the handover points between different departments or roles, and the exit points where processed documents are used for decision-making or further actions. Understanding document touchpoints enables effective integration and automation.
3. Document Capture and Ingestion: Integrate IDP systems with document capture and ingestion mechanisms to automatically capture documents from various sources. This can involve email integration, scanning devices, web-based forms, or application programming interfaces (APIs) to receive documents electronically. Streamlining document capture reduces manual

handling and enables seamless document ingestion into the IDP workflow.

4. Document Classification and Routing: Integrate the document classification and routing capabilities of IDP with the existing business processes. Route documents automatically based on their content, purpose, or other attributes to the appropriate individuals, teams, or systems. This ensures documents are directed to the right stakeholders for further processing or action.
5. Data Extraction and Validation: Integrate data extraction and validation processes within the business processes to automatically extract relevant information from documents and validate it against predefined rules. The extracted data can then be utilized for further data-driven actions or decision-making. Seamless integration of data extraction ensures accurate and timely data availability within the business processes.
6. Workflow Automation and Orchestration: Leverage workflow automation tools or business process management (BPM) systems to integrate IDP with the end-to-end business processes. Automate document routing, data extraction, validation, and approval workflows to streamline operations, reduce manual effort, and accelerate document processing. Ensure seamless handoffs and coordination between IDP and other workflow components.
7. Integration with Enterprise Systems: Integrate IDP with existing enterprise systems, such as customer relationship management (CRM), enterprise resource planning (ERP), or content management systems (CMS). Connect IDP with these systems to exchange data, update records, or trigger relevant actions based on document processing outcomes. Integration with enterprise systems enhances data flow and supports end-to-end process automation.
8. Collaboration and Communication: Integrate IDP with collaboration and communication tools to facilitate seamless collaboration among stakeholders involved in document-driven processes. Enable document sharing, real-time commenting,

task assignment, or notifications within the collaboration platforms. This fosters effective communication, improves team collaboration, and expedites decision-making.

9. Reporting and Analytics: Integrate IDP with reporting and analytics systems to gain insights into document processing performance, productivity, and outcomes. Generate meaningful reports and dashboards that provide visibility into key performance indicators (KPIs), process bottlenecks, or data quality metrics. Leveraging analytics enables data-driven decision-making and continuous process improvement.
10. Security and Compliance: Ensure secure integration by implementing appropriate security measures to protect sensitive documents and data. Incorporate access controls, encryption, user authentication, and auditing mechanisms to safeguard document integrity and maintain compliance with data protection regulations.

By integrating IDP with business processes, organizations can streamline document workflows, automate repetitive tasks, improve data accuracy, and enhance overall operational efficiency. By mapping touchpoints, capturing documents, automating document classification, routing, data extraction, and validation, organizations can achieve seamless integration and realize the full potential of IDP within their business processes.

Automating Data Transfer to Enterprise Systems (e.g., ERP, CRM)

Automating data transfer from Intelligent Document Processing (IDP) systems to enterprise systems, such as Enterprise Resource Planning (ERP) or Customer Relationship Management (CRM) platforms, enables seamless integration and facilitates end-to-end data flow within organizations. This section explores the details of automating data transfer to enterprise systems.

1. Data Mapping and Transformation: Understand the data requirements and structure of the target enterprise systems. Map the extracted data fields from IDP to the corresponding fields in the enterprise systems. Identify any necessary data

transformations, conversions, or mappings to ensure compatibility between the data extracted from documents and the data format required by the enterprise systems.

2. API Integration: Leverage application programming interfaces (APIs) provided by the target enterprise systems to establish integration channels. API integration enables direct and secure communication between the IDP system and the enterprise systems. Familiarize yourself with the APIs' functionalities, authentication mechanisms, data formats, and available endpoints for data transfer.
3. Real-Time or Batch Processing: Determine whether real-time or batch processing is suitable for data transfer, depending on the nature and urgency of the data. Real-time processing involves transferring data immediately after extraction, providing instant updates in the enterprise systems. Batch processing involves collecting a set of data over a specific time period and transferring it in bulk at regular intervals.
4. Data Validation and Preprocessing: Perform data validation and preprocessing steps before transferring data to enterprise systems. Validate the extracted data against predefined rules or business logic to ensure its accuracy, consistency, and compliance with the enterprise systems' requirements. Preprocess the data as needed, such as formatting dates, converting units, or applying data transformations, to align with the enterprise systems' data structures.
5. Error Handling and Logging: Implement error handling mechanisms to capture and handle data transfer errors or failures. Incorporate logging functionality to record the details of successful transfers and any encountered errors or exceptions. This enables effective monitoring, troubleshooting, and auditing of the data transfer process.
6. Data Synchronization: Establish mechanisms for data synchronization between the IDP system and the enterprise systems. Ensure that updates, modifications, or deletions made in either system are synchronized bidirectionally to maintain data consistency and accuracy. Determine the frequency and

timing of data synchronization based on the business needs and data dependencies.

7. Data Security and Access Controls: Implement robust data security measures during data transfer to protect sensitive information. Utilize encryption techniques, secure protocols, and access controls to ensure data confidentiality and integrity. Authenticate and authorize users or systems accessing the enterprise systems to maintain strict control over data access.
8. Data Governance and Compliance: Adhere to data governance practices and compliance requirements when transferring data to enterprise systems. Ensure that data privacy regulations, industry standards, and internal data governance policies are followed. Implement mechanisms for data masking or anonymization if required to safeguard sensitive information.
9. Logging and Monitoring: Monitor the data transfer process and log relevant information, such as transfer status, timestamps, and error details. Set up monitoring alerts or notifications to promptly address any issues or anomalies. Regularly review logs and monitoring data to identify performance bottlenecks, data inconsistencies, or system integration issues.
10. Performance Optimization: Optimize the data transfer process for efficiency and scalability. Consider techniques such as data compression, data chunking, or parallel processing to enhance performance. Fine-tune the data transfer parameters, such as batch sizes, API request limits, or network configurations, to achieve optimal performance.

By automating data transfer to enterprise systems, organizations can streamline data flow, eliminate manual data entry, reduce errors, and enhance data consistency and integrity. Automating the data transfer process enables organizations to leverage the full potential of IDP and integrate it seamlessly with their enterprise systems, fostering efficient data-driven decision-making and enhancing overall operational efficiency.

Enabling Seamless Integration with Workflow Automation Tools

Seamless integration between Intelligent Document Processing (IDP) systems and workflow automation tools enhances the efficiency and effectiveness of document-driven processes. Workflow automation tools provide a framework to design, manage, and execute end-to-end business processes, while IDP systems handle document processing tasks. This section explores the details of enabling seamless integration between IDP and workflow automation tools.

1. Understanding Workflow Requirements: Gain a comprehensive understanding of the organization's workflow requirements and existing workflow automation tools. Identify the specific processes, tasks, and document-related workflows that require integration with IDP. Analyze the input and output requirements, dependencies, and collaboration needs within the workflows.
2. Workflow Mapping and Design: Map the document-related tasks and processes within the workflows to the capabilities of the IDP system. Determine how document ingestion, classification, data extraction, validation, and routing fit into the overall workflow design. Identify the touchpoints where documents interact with different stages of the workflow and define integration points accordingly.
3. Integration via APIs or Connectors: Leverage APIs or connectors provided by the workflow automation tools to establish integration channels. APIs enable direct communication between the IDP system, and the workflow automation tools, allowing seamless data exchange and workflow orchestration. Explore the available APIs and integration capabilities of the workflow automation tools to identify the most suitable integration approach.
4. Document Handoffs and Triggers: Define document handoff points and triggers between the IDP system and the workflow automation tools. Determine how documents are transferred between the systems and the events or conditions that trigger the handoff. This can include document classification results, data extraction completion, or validation status. Ensure the necessary

data and metadata are passed between the systems to maintain process continuity.

5. Workflow Task Automation: Automate document-related tasks within the workflow automation tools using the capabilities of the IDP system. Integrate document ingestion, classification, and data extraction tasks directly into the workflow processes. Automate the assignment of tasks, notifications, or approvals based on the document processing outcomes.
6. Collaboration and Communication: Enable seamless collaboration and communication between the IDP system and the workflow automation tools. Incorporate collaboration features such as document sharing, commenting, or task assignment within the workflow automation tools. Ensure that stakeholders involved in document-related tasks can easily access and interact with the documents processed by the IDP system.
7. Error Handling and Exception Management: Implement error handling mechanisms to capture and address exceptions or errors encountered during document processing within the workflow automation tools. Define protocols for handling exceptions, such as notifications, escalations, or manual review processes. Ensure that error handling processes are integrated seamlessly into the overall workflow design.
8. Process Monitoring and Reporting: Establish monitoring and reporting capabilities to track the progress, performance, and outcomes of document-related processes within the workflow automation tools. Monitor key performance indicators (KPIs), process bottlenecks, or data quality metrics to ensure process efficiency and identify areas for improvement. Generate reports and dashboards that provide visibility into document processing status and key metrics.
9. Workflow Optimization: Continuously optimize the integrated workflow by analyzing process data, user feedback, and performance metrics. Identify opportunities for process improvement, automation, or reengineering. Fine-tune the

workflow design, document handoffs, or task assignments based on insights gained from the integrated workflow analysis.

10. Security and Access Controls: Implement security measures to ensure the confidentiality, integrity, and availability of documents and data within the integrated workflow. Apply access controls, encryption, user authentication, and audit trails to protect sensitive information. Align with data protection regulations and organizational data governance policies to maintain compliance.

Enabling seamless integration between IDP and workflow automation tools allows organizations to streamline document-driven processes, reduce manual effort, improve process visibility, and enhance overall efficiency. By mapping workflows, leveraging APIs, automating tasks, facilitating collaboration, and optimizing processes, organizations can unlock the full potential of IDP and workflow automation tools, achieving process excellence and delivering superior business outcomes.

Streamlining Collaboration and Approval Processes

Efficient collaboration and streamlined approval processes are critical components of document-driven workflows. By leveraging Intelligent Document Processing (IDP) and implementing effective collaboration and approval mechanisms, organizations can enhance teamwork, accelerate decision-making, and improve overall process efficiency. This section explores the details of streamlining collaboration and approval processes.

1. Document Sharing and Access: Implement a centralized document repository or collaboration platform to facilitate seamless document sharing and access. Ensure that relevant stakeholders can easily access and collaborate on documents within a secure and controlled environment. Utilize document versioning and access controls to maintain document integrity and prevent unauthorized access.
2. Collaboration Features: Incorporate collaboration features within the document repository or collaboration platform. Enable features such as real-time commenting, task assignment, document annotation, or document history tracking. These features facilitate effective communication, feedback exchange, and collaboration among team members.
3. Automated Task Assignment: Automate task assignment within the collaboration platform based on document processing outcomes from the IDP system. Assign tasks to the appropriate individuals or teams based on predefined rules, document types, or roles. Automating task assignment ensures efficient distribution of workload and eliminates manual assignment overhead.
4. Notification and Alert Mechanisms: Implement notification and alert mechanisms to keep stakeholders informed about document status changes, task assignments, or approval requests. Utilize email notifications, in-app notifications, or instant messaging platforms to deliver timely updates.

Notifications and alerts ensure that relevant stakeholders are aware of their responsibilities and can take prompt action.

5. Approval Workflows: Establish approval workflows within the collaboration platform to streamline the approval processes. Define approval hierarchies, routing rules, and decision criteria based on organizational policies. Automate approval requests based on document attributes or data extracted by the IDP system. This ensures a smooth and consistent approval process, reducing bottlenecks and delays.
6. Parallel and Sequential Approvals: Configure approval workflows to accommodate both parallel and sequential approvals based on business requirements. Parallel approvals allow multiple approvers to review and provide feedback simultaneously. Sequential approvals follow a specific order, where each approver reviews the document one after another. Determine the appropriate approval type based on the nature of the document and the approval process.
7. Escalation and Reminder Mechanisms: Implement escalation and reminder mechanisms to ensure timely completion of approval tasks. If an approver fails to respond within a specified timeframe, automatically escalate the approval request to the next level of authority. Send reminders to approvers for pending or upcoming approval tasks to avoid delays and improve overall process efficiency.
8. Mobile Collaboration and Approvals: Enable mobile access and collaboration capabilities to support on-the-go collaboration and approvals. Implement mobile applications or responsive web interfaces that allow stakeholders to access documents, review and approve tasks, or provide feedback from their mobile devices. Mobile access ensures flexibility, reduces response time, and enables seamless collaboration.
9. Integration with IDP and Workflow Systems: Integrate the collaboration and approval processes with the IDP system and other workflow automation tools. Connect the collaboration platform with the IDP system to enable direct access to processed documents, comments, and approval statuses. Ensure

that the collaboration platform aligns with the workflow automation tools to maintain a unified and efficient document-driven workflow.

10. Audit Trails and Document History: Maintain comprehensive audit trails and document history logs within the collaboration platform. Capture details of document activities, comments, approval decisions, and any changes made during the collaboration and approval processes. Audit trails enable traceability, accountability, and support regulatory compliance.

By streamlining collaboration and approval processes, organizations can improve communication, foster teamwork, and expedite decision-making. Leveraging collaboration platforms, automating task assignments, implementing approval workflows, and integrating with IDP and workflow systems, organizations can achieve efficient collaboration, faster approvals, and enhanced process efficiency within document-driven workflows.

Chapter 14: Advanced IDP Techniques

Overview: Chapter 14 delves into advanced Intelligent Document Processing (IDP) techniques that enable organizations to achieve even higher levels of accuracy, efficiency, and automation in document processing workflows. This chapter explores cutting-edge techniques, tools, and strategies that leverage advanced technologies to optimize IDP performance and deliver exceptional results.

1. Advanced Data Extraction Techniques: This section explores advanced data extraction techniques that go beyond traditional methods. It covers approaches such as deep learning-based extraction models, which can handle complex document structures, unstructured data, and nuanced information extraction. Advanced techniques may involve leveraging pre-trained models, transfer learning, or domain-specific models to extract information accurately and efficiently.
2. Natural Language Processing (NLP) for Document Understanding: NLP techniques enhance document understanding and enable more sophisticated data extraction. This section explores how NLP algorithms, such as sentiment analysis, entity recognition, or topic modeling, can be applied to documents to extract valuable insights, sentiments, or key information. NLP techniques enable a deeper understanding of document content and support more advanced analysis and decision-making processes.
3. Intelligent Document Classification: Advanced document classification techniques go beyond simple rule-based or keyword-based approaches. This section explores the use of machine learning algorithms, such as support vector machines, random forests, or deep learning models, to classify documents accurately based on content, context, or patterns. Advanced techniques enable more precise document classification and support complex categorization requirements.

4. Automated Document Redaction: Automated document redaction techniques enable the efficient and accurate removal of sensitive or confidential information from documents. This section explores advanced methods, such as machine learning-based redaction models or pattern recognition algorithms, that can identify and redact sensitive information with a high level of accuracy while preserving document structure and integrity.
5. Advanced Data Validation and Verification: Advanced data validation techniques focus on ensuring data accuracy and consistency. This section explores techniques such as machine learning-based anomaly detection, data matching algorithms, or semantic validation to identify data inconsistencies, outliers, or errors. Advanced validation methods enhance the reliability of extracted data and reduce manual verification efforts.
6. Intelligent Document Layout Understanding: Advanced techniques for document layout understanding involve the use of computer vision and deep learning algorithms to analyze and understand document layouts. This section explores how techniques like optical character recognition (OCR), layout analysis, or template-based parsing can be used to extract data accurately from complex document layouts, including invoices, forms, or contracts.
7. Sentiment Analysis and Document Insights: Sentiment analysis techniques enable the extraction of subjective information and opinions from documents. This section explores how sentiment analysis algorithms can be applied to understand the sentiment or emotional tone expressed within documents. Advanced techniques allow organizations to gain deeper insights into customer feedback, reviews, or social media content for improved decision-making.
8. Intelligent Document Summarization: Advanced document summarization techniques automatically generate concise summaries of large or complex documents. This section explores techniques such as extractive summarization, abstractive summarization, or deep learning-based models that can distill the most important information from documents.

Advanced summarization techniques save time, enable efficient document review, and support information retrieval.

9. Augmented Data Extraction and Human-in-the-Loop: Advanced IDP techniques incorporate human-in-the-loop processes to enhance data extraction accuracy. This section explores how human reviewers can provide feedback, validate extracted data, or handle complex cases that require human judgment. Advanced techniques leverage machine learning models that learn from human feedback, enabling continuous improvement of data extraction processes.
10. Continuous Learning and Adaptive Models: Advanced IDP systems employ continuous learning techniques to adapt to evolving document patterns and variations. This section explores how models can be continuously trained with new data, incorporate feedback loops, or leverage active learning methods to improve performance over time. Continuous learning enables IDP systems to adapt to changing document types, formats, or variations.

By exploring and implementing advanced IDP techniques, organizations can achieve higher accuracy, efficiency, and automation in their document processing workflows. Leveraging advanced data extraction, NLP, document classification, redaction, data validation, and layout understanding techniques empowers organizations to unlock the full potential of IDP and gain a competitive edge in document-driven processes.

Implementing Intelligent Redaction for Sensitive Information

Implementing intelligent redaction techniques is crucial for organizations that handle sensitive information in their document processing workflows. Intelligent redaction enables the automated identification and removal of sensitive or confidential information from documents, ensuring data privacy and compliance. This section explores the details of implementing intelligent redaction for sensitive information.

1. Define Sensitive Information: Begin by defining the types of sensitive information that need to be redacted from documents.

This may include personally identifiable information (PII), financial data, healthcare records, intellectual property, or any other confidential information specific to your organization. Understand the regulatory requirements and internal policies that govern the redaction process.

2. Machine Learning-based Redaction Models: Implement machine learning-based redaction models to automate the redaction process. Train the models using labeled datasets that contain examples of sensitive information. This enables the models to learn patterns and characteristics of sensitive data for accurate identification and redaction. Consider using techniques such as deep learning or natural language processing to enhance the model's understanding of context and improve accuracy.
3. Redaction Rules and Patterns: Establish redaction rules and patterns that guide the redaction process. These rules can be based on regular expressions, keyword matching, or predefined patterns that help identify sensitive information. Customize the rules based on the specific requirements of your organization, industry, or regulatory compliance.
4. Contextual Understanding: Enhance redaction accuracy by incorporating contextual understanding. Consider the context in which sensitive information appears within documents to avoid false positives or negatives. Analyze the surrounding text, semantic relationships, or document structure to determine whether information should be redacted. Advanced techniques such as natural language processing or machine learning models can assist in understanding context.
5. Partial Redaction and Masking: Implement partial redaction or masking techniques to preserve document readability while concealing sensitive information. Rather than completely removing sensitive data, use techniques such as blacking out, obfuscation, or replacing characters with placeholders to mask the information while maintaining the document's integrity and format.
6. Fine-tuning and Validation: Continuously fine-tune the redaction models based on feedback and validation. Regularly

review the redacted documents to ensure accuracy and assess the performance of the redaction models. Incorporate a feedback loop to capture any missed sensitive information or false positives and use this information to refine the redaction models.

7. Automation and Batch Processing: Enable automation and batch processing capabilities to efficiently handle large volumes of documents. Implement tools or workflows that allow for the automated redaction of sensitive information across multiple documents. This reduces manual effort, accelerates processing times, and ensures consistency in the redaction process.
8. Audit Trails and Documentation: Maintain detailed audit trails and documentation of the redaction process. Document the redaction rules, patterns, and criteria used to ensure transparency and compliance. Keep records of redacted documents, including the date, time, and rationale for redaction, as well as any approvals or reviews conducted during the process.
9. Compliance and Data Protection: Ensure compliance with relevant regulations, such as the General Data Protection Regulation (GDPR) or industry-specific data protection requirements. Understand the legal and regulatory obligations for redacting sensitive information and ensure that your redaction process aligns with these requirements. Implement security measures to protect redacted documents and ensure that access to sensitive data is restricted to authorized personnel.
10. Ongoing Training and Evaluation: Continuously train and evaluate the redaction models to improve performance over time. Incorporate new data, feedback from reviewers, or changes in sensitive information patterns into the training process. Regularly assess the effectiveness of the redaction process and make adjustments as necessary to maintain accuracy and compliance.

By implementing intelligent redaction techniques, organizations can protect sensitive information, maintain data privacy, and comply with regulatory requirements. Leveraging machine learning-based redaction models, contextual understanding, partial redaction, and automation capabilities, organizations can achieve efficient and accurate redaction of sensitive information within their document processing workflows.

Applying Sentiment Analysis to Extract Insights from Text

Sentiment analysis is a powerful technique that enables organizations to extract valuable insights from textual data by determining the sentiment or emotional tone expressed within the text. By applying sentiment analysis to text documents, organizations can gain a deeper understanding of customer feedback, social media content, reviews, or any other form of textual data. This section explores the details of applying sentiment analysis to extract insights from text.

1. Sentiment Analysis Basics: Understand the fundamentals of sentiment analysis, which involves using natural language processing (NLP) techniques to automatically classify text into positive, negative, or neutral sentiments. Sentiment analysis algorithms can analyze text at the document, sentence, or even entity level, providing an overall sentiment score or sentiment distribution.
2. Text Preprocessing: Perform text preprocessing steps to clean and prepare the text for sentiment analysis. This may involve removing irrelevant information such as punctuation, stop words, or special characters. Additionally, techniques like stemming, lemmatization, or spell-checking can help standardize the text and improve sentiment analysis accuracy.
3. Lexicon-based Approaches: Lexicon-based sentiment analysis utilizes pre-built sentiment lexicons or dictionaries containing words or phrases along with their associated sentiment scores. Words are matched against the lexicon, and sentiment scores are aggregated to determine the overall sentiment of the text. Lexicons can be general-purpose or domain-specific, allowing customization for specific industries or contexts.

4. Machine Learning-based Approaches: Machine learning algorithms, such as support vector machines, decision trees, or deep learning models, can be applied for sentiment analysis. These algorithms learn patterns and relationships from labeled training data, enabling them to classify unseen text based on learned patterns. Machine learning-based approaches can achieve high accuracy and handle complex language nuances.
5. Aspect-based Sentiment Analysis: Aspect-based sentiment analysis delves deeper into the sentiment expressed towards specific aspects or entities within the text. It identifies and analyzes sentiments associated with different aspects, such as product features, service components, or specific topics. This provides a more granular understanding of sentiment and enables organizations to address specific areas for improvement.
6. Entity-level Sentiment Analysis: Entity-level sentiment analysis focuses on identifying sentiments expressed towards individual entities mentioned in the text, such as brands, products, or people. It helps organizations gauge public perception, customer sentiment, or sentiment trends associated with specific entities. This information can inform product development, marketing strategies, or customer relationship management efforts.
7. Emotion Analysis: Sentiment analysis can be extended to analyze emotions expressed within the text. Emotion analysis techniques identify and classify emotions such as joy, anger, fear, or sadness. This provides insights into the emotional state of individuals or the general sentiment surrounding a particular topic or event.
8. Customization and Training: Customize sentiment analysis models based on industry-specific or organization-specific requirements. Fine-tune models using labeled datasets that align with the specific domain or context of the text. Training models on industry-specific data enhances the accuracy and relevance of sentiment analysis results.
9. Integration with Other Systems: Integrate sentiment analysis with other systems or applications to leverage the extracted insights effectively. For example, sentiment analysis results can

be incorporated into customer relationship management (CRM) systems to assess customer satisfaction or into social media monitoring tools to track public sentiment towards a brand or product.

10. Continuous Improvement: Continuously evaluate and improve sentiment analysis models based on feedback and validation. Monitor model performance, identify misclassifications or areas for improvement, and incorporate user feedback to refine the sentiment analysis process. Keep models up-to-date with changing language trends, customer preferences, or emerging sentiments.

By applying sentiment analysis to text documents, organizations can gain valuable insights into customer sentiment, public perception, or emotional trends. Leveraging lexicon-based or machine learning-based approaches, aspect-based or entity-level analysis, and customizing models for specific domains, organizations can make informed decisions, improve products or services, and enhance customer experiences.

Leveraging IDP for Regulatory Compliance (e.g., KYC, AML)

Intelligent Document Processing (IDP) can play a crucial role in facilitating regulatory compliance for various industries, particularly in areas such as Know Your Customer (KYC) and Anti-Money Laundering (AML) processes. By automating document verification, data extraction, and risk assessment, IDP can help organizations efficiently meet regulatory requirements and enhance compliance efforts. This section explores the details of leveraging IDP for regulatory compliance.

1. KYC and Customer Onboarding: IDP can streamline the KYC process by automating the collection and verification of customer identity documents. By extracting relevant data from documents such as passports, driver's licenses, or ID cards, IDP can automate identity verification, perform risk assessments, and ensure compliance with KYC regulations. IDP enables faster and more accurate customer onboarding while reducing manual effort.

2. AML and Transaction Monitoring: IDP can assist organizations in detecting and preventing money laundering activities through efficient document processing and data extraction. By automating the extraction of key information from transaction-related documents, such as invoices, contracts, or financial statements, IDP can facilitate enhanced transaction monitoring. It can identify suspicious patterns, perform risk assessments, and flag potentially fraudulent activities for further investigation.
3. Regulatory Reporting: IDP can simplify the process of generating regulatory reports by automating data extraction and analysis. By extracting relevant information from documents, such as transaction records or customer profiles, IDP can facilitate the compilation of accurate and comprehensive regulatory reports. This helps organizations meet reporting obligations more efficiently, ensuring compliance with regulatory requirements.
4. Risk Assessment and Due Diligence: IDP can aid in risk assessment and due diligence processes by automating the extraction and analysis of data from various documents. It can assess customer profiles, financial statements, or business contracts to identify potential risks, verify information, and support compliance with regulatory standards. IDP enhances the accuracy and efficiency of risk assessment, enabling organizations to make informed decisions.
5. Fraud Detection and Prevention: IDP can assist in fraud detection and prevention by automating the extraction and analysis of data from documents associated with potentially fraudulent activities. By identifying inconsistencies, anomalies, or suspicious patterns in documents, such as invoices, receipts, or transaction records, IDP can help organizations detect and prevent fraudulent behavior. It enhances the effectiveness of fraud monitoring and contributes to regulatory compliance.
6. Document Retention and Audit Trails: IDP can support document retention and audit trail requirements, which are critical for regulatory compliance. By capturing and storing

processed documents, along with associated metadata and audit logs, IDP enables organizations to maintain a complete record of document processing activities. This ensures transparency, accountability, and supports compliance audits or investigations.

7. Data Privacy and Protection: IDP should incorporate robust data privacy and protection measures to ensure compliance with data protection regulations, such as the General Data Protection Regulation (GDPR). Implement encryption, access controls, data anonymization, or pseudonymization techniques to safeguard sensitive information contained in documents. By protecting customer data and ensuring data privacy, IDP supports regulatory compliance efforts.
8. Integration with Compliance Systems: Integrate IDP with compliance systems, such as AML platforms or compliance management tools, to enable seamless data exchange and process integration. This allows organizations to leverage the extracted data and insights from IDP for enhanced risk assessment, compliance monitoring, or reporting. Integration ensures that IDP complements existing compliance frameworks and systems.
9. Continuous Monitoring and Adaptation: Continuously monitor and adapt IDP processes to align with changing regulatory requirements. Stay updated with regulatory changes, updates, or new compliance standards relevant to your industry. Regularly evaluate the effectiveness of IDP in meeting compliance goals and make necessary adjustments to maintain accuracy, relevancy, and compliance with evolving regulations.
10. Compliance Training and Governance: Ensure that employees involved in IDP processes receive adequate training on regulatory compliance requirements. Establish governance mechanisms, policies, and procedures to oversee the IDP implementation and compliance activities. Regularly conduct internal audits or assessments to monitor the effectiveness of IDP in meeting compliance objectives.

By leveraging IDP for regulatory compliance, organizations can streamline KYC processes, enhance AML efforts, improve risk assessments, and strengthen compliance monitoring. Implementing IDP ensures accuracy, efficiency, and automation in document processing, contributing to effective regulatory compliance and mitigating legal and financial risks.

CHAPTER 15: MONITORING AND MEASURING IDP PERFORMANCE

Overview: Chapter 15 focuses on monitoring and measuring the performance of Intelligent Document Processing (IDP) systems. Monitoring and measuring IDP performance are essential to ensure accuracy, efficiency, and continuous improvement in document processing workflows. This chapter provides an overview of key metrics, monitoring techniques, and strategies to evaluate and optimize IDP performance.

1. Key Performance Indicators (KPIs): Define relevant KPIs to monitor and measure the performance of the IDP system. These KPIs may include accuracy metrics such as extraction accuracy, classification accuracy, or error rates. Efficiency metrics such as processing time, throughput, or document processing volume are also crucial. Additionally, consider metrics related to customer satisfaction, data quality, or compliance to assess the overall impact of IDP.
2. Real-time Monitoring: Implement real-time monitoring mechanisms to track IDP performance. Use dashboards, alerts, or notifications to gain real-time insights into system health, processing status, or exceptions. Real-time monitoring allows for prompt response to issues, enables proactive decision-making, and facilitates efficient resource allocation.
3. Data Sampling and Validation: Perform data sampling and validation to assess the accuracy and reliability of the IDP system. Select a representative sample of processed documents and manually validate the results against ground truth or expert judgment. This validation process helps identify any discrepancies, assess error rates, and validate the performance of the IDP system.
4. Error Analysis and Root Cause Identification: Conduct error analysis to identify the root causes of inaccuracies or processing

errors. Analyze the types of errors, their frequency, and the underlying reasons behind them. This analysis helps pinpoint areas of improvement, identify common error patterns, and guide targeted enhancements in document classification, data extraction, or validation processes.

5. Continuous Improvement Feedback Loop: Establish a feedback loop for continuous improvement. Encourage users and stakeholders to provide feedback on IDP performance, usability, or any encountered issues. Collect feedback on false positives, false negatives, or any areas where the IDP system may require adjustments. Incorporate this feedback into system enhancements, training data improvements, or model refinement to drive continuous improvement.
6. Benchmarking and Comparison: Benchmark the performance of the IDP system against industry standards or internal benchmarks. Compare the IDP system's performance with similar systems or alternative approaches to identify areas of competitive advantage or improvement opportunities. Benchmarking enables organizations to set realistic performance goals, track progress, and drive continuous optimization.
7. Scalability and Performance Optimization: Assess the scalability of the IDP system to handle increasing document volumes or processing demands. Monitor system performance under various loads and evaluate response times, throughput, and resource utilization. Optimize system parameters, infrastructure, or parallel processing capabilities to ensure smooth scalability and efficient performance.
8. User Experience and Feedback: Consider the user experience as a key aspect of IDP performance. Gather feedback from users, administrators, or other stakeholders involved in the IDP process. Evaluate their satisfaction, ease of use, and the impact of the IDP system on their daily operations. Incorporate user feedback into system enhancements, interface improvements, or usability optimizations.
9. Compliance and Audit Readiness: Ensure the IDP system complies with relevant regulatory requirements and supports

audit readiness. Monitor and track compliance-related metrics, such as accuracy of redaction, data protection measures, or audit trail completeness. Regularly conduct internal audits to assess compliance and implement necessary adjustments to ensure adherence to regulations.

10. Reporting and Analytics: Generate comprehensive reports and analytics to communicate IDP performance and insights to stakeholders. Provide detailed performance metrics, trend analysis, and visualizations to highlight areas of success, improvement, or compliance. Use analytics to identify patterns, make data-driven decisions, and communicate the value and impact of IDP within the organization.

Monitoring and measuring IDP performance allows organizations to evaluate the effectiveness of their document processing workflows, identify areas for improvement, and drive continuous optimization. By monitoring key metrics, conducting error analysis, leveraging user feedback, and implementing scalability strategies, organizations can ensure that their IDP system performs optimally and delivers the desired outcomes.

Setting Up Performance Metrics and Monitoring Tools

Setting up performance metrics and monitoring tools is crucial for effectively evaluating and optimizing the performance of an Intelligent Document Processing (IDP) system. These metrics and tools provide insights into system efficiency, accuracy, throughput, and other critical aspects of document processing workflows. This section explores the details of setting up performance metrics and monitoring tools for IDP.

1. Define Relevant Performance Metrics: Start by defining the performance metrics that align with your organization's goals and objectives. Consider metrics such as accuracy rates, error rates, processing time, throughput (number of documents processed per unit of time), document processing volume, or customer satisfaction metrics. Ensure that the metrics selected are measurable, meaningful, and aligned with the specific outcomes you aim to achieve.

2. Establish Baseline Metrics: Establish baseline metrics by capturing performance data from the existing document processing workflows before implementing the IDP system. This provides a benchmark for comparison and helps evaluate the impact of IDP implementation on performance. Baseline metrics serve as a reference point for measuring improvements and assessing the effectiveness of the IDP system.
3. Automated Performance Monitoring: Implement automated performance monitoring tools that track and capture relevant performance data in real-time. These tools can monitor system health, processing status, errors, or other key performance indicators. Automated monitoring allows for proactive identification of issues, timely responses, and continuous tracking of performance trends.
4. Data Sampling and Validation: Perform data sampling and validation to assess the accuracy and reliability of the IDP system's performance metrics. Select a representative sample of processed documents and compare the extracted data against ground truth or expert validation. This validation process helps identify any discrepancies, validate the accuracy of the IDP system's output, and ensure the reliability of performance metrics.
5. Data Visualization and Dashboards: Utilize data visualization techniques and dashboards to present performance metrics in a clear and intuitive manner. Visual representations, such as charts, graphs, or heatmaps, help stakeholders understand performance trends, identify patterns, and make informed decisions. Dashboards provide a centralized view of performance metrics, enabling stakeholders to monitor and analyze performance easily.
6. Alerts and Notifications: Implement alerts and notifications to proactively monitor performance deviations or critical issues. Set up thresholds or triggers that generate alerts when performance metrics fall outside acceptable ranges or when errors occur. These alerts allow immediate attention and prompt

action to address performance issues and minimize potential disruptions.

7. Regular Performance Analysis: Conduct regular performance analysis to identify areas for improvement and optimization. Analyze performance metrics, review trends, and compare against established benchmarks or targets. Identify any bottlenecks, patterns of errors, or areas where performance falls short. Regular analysis provides insights for fine-tuning the IDP system, optimizing processes, or addressing any performance gaps.
8. Integration with Logging and Audit Trails: Integrate performance metrics with logging mechanisms and audit trails to maintain a comprehensive record of performance data. Capture relevant data points and system events to support performance analysis, troubleshooting, or compliance requirements. Integration ensures that performance metrics are aligned with other system-level data and can be cross-referenced for comprehensive analysis.
9. Performance Reviews and Feedback Loops: Conduct performance reviews and establish feedback loops with stakeholders to gather insights and perspectives on IDP performance. Seek feedback from end-users, administrators, or quality assurance teams to understand their experiences, identify pain points, and gather suggestions for improvement. Performance reviews and feedback loops facilitate continuous improvement and user-centric optimizations.
   10. Continuous Optimization: Continuously optimize the IDP system based on performance metrics and feedback. Leverage performance insights to make informed decisions regarding system enhancements, process streamlining, or infrastructure upgrades. Regularly assess the effectiveness of performance optimizations and fine-tune the system to align with evolving business needs and performance goals.

Setting up performance metrics and monitoring tools allows organizations to gain visibility

Analyzing Performance Data and Identifying Bottlenecks

Analyzing performance data and identifying bottlenecks is essential for optimizing the performance of an Intelligent Document Processing (IDP) system. By analyzing performance data, organizations can gain insights into system efficiency, identify areas of improvement, and address bottlenecks that hinder optimal performance. This section explores the details of analyzing performance data and identifying bottlenecks in an IDP system.

1. Collect Relevant Performance Data: Collect comprehensive performance data from the IDP system, including metrics such as processing time, error rates, throughput, resource utilization, or any other relevant indicators. Ensure that the data collection process captures a representative sample of document processing activities to provide an accurate representation of system performance.
2. Use Statistical Analysis: Apply statistical analysis techniques to the collected performance data to identify patterns, trends, or anomalies. Use descriptive statistics, such as mean, median, or standard deviation, to summarize performance metrics. Conduct hypothesis testing or correlation analysis to determine relationships between performance metrics and system variables. Statistical analysis provides quantitative insights into system performance.
3. Compare Against Benchmarks or Targets: Compare performance data against established benchmarks, targets, or industry standards to assess performance relative to desired goals. Use historical data, industry benchmarks, or best practices as reference points. Comparisons help identify performance gaps, areas for improvement, or opportunities for optimization.
4. Visualize Performance Data: Visualize performance data using charts, graphs, or visual representations to facilitate understanding and analysis. Visualizations can reveal patterns, trends, or outliers that may not be apparent in raw data. Use tools like line charts, histograms, or heatmaps to visually

represent performance metrics. Visualization aids in identifying performance patterns and drawing meaningful insights.

5. Identify Performance Bottlenecks: Analyze performance data to identify bottlenecks, which are areas where system performance is hindered or constrained. Bottlenecks may occur in various aspects of the IDP system, such as data ingestion, document preprocessing, classification, data extraction, or integration with downstream systems. Look for metrics that consistently underperform or cause delays in the document processing workflow.
6. Root Cause Analysis: Conduct root cause analysis to determine the underlying reasons behind performance bottlenecks. Investigate factors that contribute to performance issues, such as system configuration, network latency, computational resources, or data quality. Explore potential causes and conduct targeted investigations to identify the root causes of bottlenecks.
7. Collaborate with Key Stakeholders: Engage key stakeholders, including system administrators, developers, or end-users, to gather insights and perspectives on performance bottlenecks. Seek input from individuals who have firsthand experience with the IDP system to understand their observations, challenges, or pain points. Collaborative discussions help uncover performance bottlenecks that may have been overlooked.
8. Prioritize and Mitigate Bottlenecks: Prioritize identified bottlenecks based on their impact and feasibility of mitigation. Determine whether bottlenecks are related to system architecture, infrastructure, configuration, algorithms, or data quality. Develop action plans to address the identified bottlenecks and implement targeted improvements or optimizations.
9. Monitor and Evaluate Performance Improvements: Implement the necessary changes to mitigate bottlenecks and monitor the impact of improvements on performance metrics. Continuously track and evaluate performance data to assess the effectiveness of the implemented solutions. Adjustments may be required

based on iterative feedback and ongoing performance monitoring.

10. Continuous Performance Optimization: Performance optimization is an ongoing process. Regularly review performance data, assess system enhancements, and identify new potential bottlenecks as the system evolves or document processing requirements change. Continuously optimize the IDP system to ensure optimal performance and support evolving business needs.

By analyzing performance data and identifying bottlenecks, organizations can optimize their IDP systems, improve efficiency, and enhance document processing workflows. Addressing bottlenecks improves system performance, reduces processing time, and enables organizations to leverage the full potential of IDP to streamline document processing and achieve business objectives.

Implementing Continuous Improvement Initiatives

Implementing continuous improvement initiatives is crucial for organizations to optimize their Intelligent Document Processing (IDP) systems and ensure ongoing enhancements in document processing workflows. Continuous improvement drives efficiency, accuracy, and customer satisfaction while enabling organizations to adapt to evolving business needs. This section explores the details of implementing continuous improvement initiatives for IDP.

1. Establish a Culture of Continuous Improvement: Foster a culture of continuous improvement within the organization. Encourage employees at all levels to actively contribute ideas, share feedback, and participate in improvement initiatives. Create an environment where continuous improvement is valued and supported by leadership.
2. Define Improvement Goals and Objectives: Clearly define improvement goals and objectives that align with the organization's strategic vision and IDP system's performance requirements. Focus on specific areas such as accuracy, processing time, customer satisfaction, or compliance. Set measurable targets to track progress and ensure alignment with overall business objectives.
3. Regular Performance Assessment: Regularly assess the performance of the IDP system against established performance metrics and targets. Conduct periodic reviews, analyze performance data, and evaluate the effectiveness of implemented improvements. Use the insights gained from performance assessments to identify areas for further optimization.
4. Collect and Analyze User Feedback: Gather feedback from end-users, administrators, or other stakeholders involved in the IDP process. Seek insights on usability, functionality, or any pain points experienced during document processing. Analyze user

feedback to identify areas of improvement, understand user needs, and drive user-centric enhancements.

5. Monitor Industry Best Practices: Stay informed about industry best practices, emerging technologies, and advancements in the field of IDP. Monitor industry publications, attend conferences, participate in forums, or engage with industry experts to keep up to date with the latest trends. Incorporate relevant best practices into the continuous improvement initiatives.
6. Implement Process Automation: Identify opportunities to automate manual tasks within the document processing workflow. Integrate automation tools, robotic process automation (RPA), or workflow automation platforms to streamline repetitive or time-consuming activities. Automation reduces errors, enhances efficiency, and frees up resources for more value-added tasks.
7. Leverage Machine Learning and AI: Leverage machine learning and artificial intelligence techniques to enhance IDP performance. Explore advanced algorithms, such as deep learning models, to improve document classification, data extraction, or error detection. Continuously train and refine machine learning models based on new data and feedback to drive ongoing improvements.
8. Regularly Update Training Data: Regularly update and refine the training data used for machine learning models. Incorporate new samples, diverse document types, or edge cases to improve the model's accuracy and performance. Collect feedback from reviewers, validate the training data, and ensure it represents the evolving nature of document processing requirements.
9. Encourage Cross-Functional Collaboration: Promote collaboration between different teams involved in the IDP process, such as IT, operations, compliance, and business units. Foster cross-functional discussions, share knowledge, and leverage diverse perspectives to identify improvement opportunities, solve complex challenges, and drive collective ownership of continuous improvement initiatives.

10. Monitor Technology Advances: Monitor technological advancements in the IDP domain, such as advancements in OCR technologies, NLP techniques, or data extraction algorithms. Stay abreast of new tools, platforms, or APIs that can enhance IDP capabilities. Evaluate the potential benefits of adopting new technologies and incorporate them into the continuous improvement roadmap.
11. Test and Pilot New Ideas: Test and pilot new improvement ideas in controlled environments or smaller-scale projects before full-scale implementation. Conduct feasibility studies, assess risks, and measure the impact of proposed improvements. Use the insights gained from testing and piloting to refine the improvement initiatives and ensure successful implementation.
12. Continuously Train and Educate Users: Provide regular training and education sessions to users and stakeholders involved in the IDP process. Keep them informed about system updates, new features, or best practices. Foster a learning environment that encourages users to optimize their usage of the IDP system and maximize its benefits.
13. Document and Share Best Practices: Document best practices, lessons learned, and successful improvement initiatives. Create a knowledge repository or internal platform to share insights, case studies, or success stories. Encourage the exchange of ideas and facilitate cross-learning within the organization.
14. Monitor ROI and Business Impact: Monitor the return on investment (ROI) and business impact resulting from continuous improvement initiatives. Track key performance indicators related to cost savings, efficiency gains, error reduction, or customer satisfaction. Quantify the benefits achieved through continuous improvement efforts to justify investments and drive further improvements.

By implementing continuous improvement initiatives, organizations can ensure that their IDP systems remain effective, efficient, and aligned with evolving business needs. Continuous improvement fosters innovation, enables operational excellence, and drives sustainable success in document processing workflows.

CHAPTER 16: CHANGE MANAGEMENT AND USER ADOPTION

Overview: Chapter 16 focuses on change management and user adoption strategies for implementing an Intelligent Document Processing (IDP) system. Change management is crucial for successful adoption and utilization of IDP, as it involves transitioning from traditional document processing methods to automated and intelligent workflows. This chapter provides an overview of change management principles, user adoption strategies, and best practices to facilitate a smooth transition to IDP.

1. Understand the Need for Change: Begin by understanding and communicating the need for change. Clearly articulate the benefits and advantages of implementing IDP, such as improved efficiency, accuracy, compliance, or cost savings. Communicate the vision and strategic goals of the IDP initiative to create awareness and generate buy-in from stakeholders.
2. Stakeholder Engagement: Identify and engage key stakeholders who will be affected by the IDP implementation. This includes end-users, managers, IT teams, compliance officers, and other relevant parties. Involve stakeholders early in the process, seek their input, address concerns, and emphasize their role in the success of the IDP initiative. Foster a sense of ownership and collaboration.
3. Develop a Change Management Plan: Create a comprehensive change management plan that outlines the steps, milestones, and strategies for implementing IDP. Include communication strategies, training programs, and user support mechanisms in the plan. Define roles and responsibilities, set realistic timelines, and allocate resources accordingly. The change management plan should address the unique needs and challenges of the organization.

4. Communicate Effectively: Implement a robust communication strategy to keep stakeholders informed and engaged throughout the change process. Clearly communicate the objectives, benefits, and progress of the IDP implementation. Tailor messages to different stakeholder groups and use various channels such as emails, meetings, newsletters, or intranet portals to ensure widespread understanding and acceptance.
5. Training and Education: Provide comprehensive training programs to ensure users understand the functionality and benefits of the IDP system. Offer hands-on training sessions, workshops, or webinars to familiarize users with the new tools, processes, and interfaces. Tailor training programs to different user roles and skill levels. Encourage continuous learning and provide ongoing support as users adapt to the new workflows.
6. User Support: Establish a user support system to address questions, concerns, and challenges that arise during the transition to IDP. Assign dedicated support staff or helpdesk resources to assist users with technical issues, process inquiries, or system-related concerns. Provide documentation, FAQs, or knowledge bases to empower users to troubleshoot common problems.
7. Pilot and Feedback Loops: Consider piloting the IDP system in a controlled environment or with a specific user group before full-scale implementation. Gather feedback from users and incorporate their suggestions to refine the system, user interfaces, or workflows. Use pilot projects as opportunities to identify potential challenges, fine-tune processes, and build confidence among users.
8. Change Champions: Identify change champions within the organization who can advocate for the IDP system, motivate others, and share success stories. These change champions can serve as role models, provide guidance, and address concerns from their peers. Empower them with the necessary knowledge and resources to drive user adoption and promote a positive change culture.

9. Monitor User Adoption: Monitor and track user adoption of the IDP system throughout the implementation process. Collect user feedback, conduct surveys, or analyze system usage data to assess user acceptance, identify adoption barriers, and measure the effectiveness of change management strategies. Continuously evaluate user satisfaction and address any gaps or challenges proactively.
10. Continuous Improvement: Implement a feedback loop and continuous improvement process to enhance user adoption and address evolving needs. Solicit feedback from users on an ongoing basis, prioritize improvement opportunities, and make iterative adjustments to the IDP system, training programs, or support mechanisms. Continuously assess user adoption to ensure long-term success.

By focusing on change management and user adoption, organizations can facilitate a smooth transition to an IDP system. Effective communication, comprehensive training, user support, and continuous improvement efforts create a positive environment for embracing the benefits of automation and intelligent document processing.

Preparing Employees for IDP Implementation

Implementing an Intelligent Document Processing (IDP) system requires thorough preparation and effective employee readiness. Proper training and education are essential to ensure employees understand the benefits, functionalities, and workflows associated with the new system. This section provides details on preparing employees for IDP implementation.

1. Communicate the Purpose and Benefits: Clearly communicate the purpose and benefits of implementing IDP to employees. Explain how the new system will enhance efficiency, accuracy, compliance, and their overall work experience. Emphasize the positive impact it will have on their day-to-day tasks and the organization as a whole. Address any concerns or misconceptions they may have.
2. Develop a Training Plan: Create a comprehensive training plan that caters to different employee roles and skill levels. Identify the specific training needs of each group, such as end-users, managers, or IT personnel. Determine the appropriate training methods, whether it is classroom-style sessions, hands-on workshops, e-learning modules, or a combination of approaches. Consider providing refresher training as needed.
3. Customize Training Content: Tailor training content to the specific needs and processes of the organization. Develop training materials that reflect the organization's document management workflows, document types, and system interfaces. Incorporate real-life scenarios and examples to make the training relevant and practical for employees.
4. Hands-on Training: Provide hands-on training opportunities to allow employees to practice using the IDP system in a controlled environment. Simulate document processing workflows, data extraction exercises, or classification tasks to familiarize employees with the functionalities and features of the system. This practical experience helps build confidence and competence.

5. Train Super Users and Champions: Identify and train a group of super users or champions who will become experts in using the IDP system. These individuals can then serve as internal resources to provide support, answer questions, and assist other employees during and after the implementation. Invest in their training and provide ongoing support to ensure they have the knowledge and skills to guide their colleagues.
6. Emphasize User Experience: Highlight the user-friendly aspects of the IDP system and how it simplifies document processing tasks. Emphasize how the system will streamline workflows, automate repetitive tasks, and provide a more intuitive and efficient user experience. Help employees understand how the system will make their jobs easier and more productive.
7. Address Change Management: Prepare employees for the changes that accompany the implementation of IDP. Explain the reasons behind the change, address potential resistance, and provide guidance on managing the transition. Offer support mechanisms to address concerns and questions, and ensure that employees feel supported throughout the change process.
8. Ongoing Support and Resources: Establish ongoing support mechanisms, such as a dedicated helpdesk or support team, to address employee questions and provide assistance after the implementation. Develop a repository of resources, such as user guides, FAQs, or video tutorials, that employees can access as a reference whenever needed. Foster a culture of continuous learning and encourage employees to share their experiences and best practices.
9. Encourage Feedback and Collaboration: Encourage employees to provide feedback on the IDP system, share their experiences, and suggest areas for improvement. Foster a collaborative environment where employees feel comfortable expressing their opinions and contributing to the optimization of the system. Actively seek their input during the implementation and post-implementation phases.

   10. Monitor and Evaluate User Adoption: Regularly monitor and evaluate user adoption and satisfaction with the IDP system.

Collect feedback through surveys, interviews, or focus groups to identify areas where additional support or training may be needed. Measure the system's impact on productivity, accuracy, and user satisfaction to quantify the benefits of the IDP implementation.

By adequately preparing employees for IDP implementation through effective communication, tailored training programs, ongoing support, and opportunities for collaboration, organizations can ensure a successful transition and maximize the benefits of the new system.

Conducting User Training and Education Programs

User training and education programs are essential for ensuring a smooth and successful transition to an Intelligent Document Processing (IDP) system. These programs aim to equip users with the knowledge and skills required to effectively utilize the new system and optimize their document processing workflows. This section provides details on conducting user training and education programs for IDP implementation.

1. Identify User Groups and Training Needs: Identify the different user groups within the organization that will interact with the IDP system, such as end-users, managers, administrators, or IT personnel. Assess their specific training needs based on their roles, responsibilities, and familiarity with document processing workflows. Determine the appropriate level of training required for each group.
2. Define Training Objectives: Establish clear training objectives that align with the goals of the IDP implementation. Outline the specific knowledge and skills that users should acquire through the training programs. These objectives may include understanding the system's functionalities, navigating the user interface, performing document classification, data extraction, or troubleshooting common issues.
3. Develop Training Materials: Develop comprehensive training materials that cater to the identified user groups and training objectives. This may include user manuals, step-by-step guides,

video tutorials, or interactive e-learning modules. Ensure that the materials are clear, concise, and easy to follow, incorporating visuals, examples, and real-life scenarios to enhance understanding.

4. Select Training Methods: Choose the appropriate training methods that best suit the organization's needs and user preferences. Consider a mix of training approaches, such as instructor-led sessions, hands-on workshops, virtual classrooms, webinars, or self-paced e-learning modules. Tailor the training methods to accommodate different learning styles and the availability of resources.
5. Conduct Hands-on Training: Provide hands-on training opportunities that allow users to practice using the IDP system in a simulated environment. This enables users to familiarize themselves with system functionalities, perform tasks, and gain confidence in their abilities. Create exercises and scenarios that replicate real-life document processing workflows to ensure practical application of the learned concepts.
6. Leverage Real Document Examples: Incorporate real document examples that users encounter in their daily work into the training programs. Use these examples to demonstrate how to effectively classify documents, extract data, and handle different document formats. By using familiar documents, users can easily relate to the training material and understand how to apply the IDP system to their specific needs.
7. Provide Role-Based Training: Tailor training programs to specific user roles or departments to address their unique requirements. Customize the training content and scenarios to reflect the workflows, document types, and challenges relevant to each user group. This approach ensures that users receive targeted training that directly relates to their job responsibilities and enhances their efficiency.
8. Schedule Training Sessions: Plan and schedule training sessions well in advance to ensure user availability and participation. Provide a variety of training session options, considering different shifts, remote locations, or time zones, if applicable.

Communicate the training schedule clearly to all users and provide reminders to ensure maximum attendance.

9. Offer Ongoing Support: Establish a support mechanism to assist users during and after the training programs. Provide contact information for a helpdesk or dedicated support personnel who can address user questions, provide guidance, and troubleshoot issues. Offer a support portal or knowledge base where users can access resources, FAQs, or troubleshooting guides at their convenience.
10. Evaluate Training Effectiveness: Evaluate the effectiveness of the training programs by conducting post-training assessments or surveys to gather user feedback. Assess user comprehension, confidence levels, and the ability to apply the learned skills in their daily work. Use this feedback to identify areas for improvement in training materials, methodologies, or ongoing support.
11. Encourage Continuous Learning: Promote a culture of continuous learning and skill development by providing resources for users to further enhance their IDP knowledge. Offer advanced training sessions, webinars, or workshops for users who want to deepen their understanding or expand their capabilities with the IDP system. Encourage sharing of best practices and peer-to-peer learning within the organization.

By conducting user training and education programs, organizations can empower users to fully leverage the capabilities of the IDP system, enhance their proficiency in document processing, and achieve optimal results in their work.

Addressing Change Resistance and Overcoming Challenges

During the implementation of an Intelligent Document Processing (IDP) system, organizations may encounter resistance to change and face various challenges. It is essential to proactively address these issues to ensure successful adoption and maximize the benefits of IDP. This section provides details on addressing change resistance and overcoming challenges during the IDP implementation process.

1. Understand the Root Causes of Resistance: Take the time to understand the reasons behind resistance to change. Common causes may include fear of job loss, lack of understanding of the benefits, concerns about competence with new technology, or the perception of increased workload. Conduct surveys, interviews, or focus groups to gather insights from employees and identify the specific areas of resistance.
2. Communicate the Vision and Benefits: Communicate the vision and benefits of IDP clearly and consistently. Emphasize how the new system will improve efficiency, accuracy, compliance, and job satisfaction. Tailor the communication to address the concerns and motivations of different stakeholder groups. Demonstrate how IDP aligns with the organization's strategic goals and supports employees in their work.
3. Provide Training and Support: Offer comprehensive training programs to equip employees with the knowledge and skills required to use the IDP system effectively. Ensure that employees feel supported during the transition by providing ongoing training and support mechanisms, such as dedicated helpdesk resources, user guides, or FAQs. Address any knowledge gaps or uncertainties that may contribute to resistance.
4. Identify Change Champions: Identify influential individuals or change champions within the organization who can advocate for IDP and help overcome resistance. These change champions can serve as role models, share success stories, and provide guidance and support to their colleagues. Engage them in the implementation process and encourage them to actively address concerns and promote the benefits of IDP.
5. Involve Employees in the Process: Involve employees in the IDP implementation process by seeking their input, feedback, and suggestions. Engage them in decision-making, system testing, or process improvement initiatives. This participation creates a sense of ownership, increases their commitment to the change, and reduces resistance.

6. Address Training and Support Needs: Ensure that employees have access to the necessary training and support to navigate the IDP system. Address any gaps in knowledge or skills through additional training sessions, workshops, or one-on-one coaching. Provide ongoing support and resources to address any challenges that arise during the transition period.
7. Foster a Learning Culture: Create a learning culture that encourages continuous learning and growth. Offer opportunities for employees to expand their knowledge of IDP through seminars, webinars, or conferences. Provide resources such as online courses, documentation, or knowledge-sharing platforms to support their development. Recognize and reward employees who embrace the change and actively seek improvement.
8. Address Fear of Job Loss: Address concerns related to job security by emphasizing how IDP enhances employees' roles rather than replacing them. Highlight the value of human judgment, decision-making, and creativity in combination with the capabilities of the IDP system. Emphasize how IDP can free up time for more meaningful tasks and allow employees to focus on higher-value activities.
9. Monitor and Address Performance Issues: Monitor the performance of the IDP system and address any issues promptly. If employees experience technical difficulties or encounter challenges with the system, provide quick resolutions and communicate updates transparently. Addressing performance issues promptly helps maintain employee confidence in the new system and minimizes disruption to their work.

10. Celebrate Success and Share Wins: Recognize and celebrate early successes and achievements resulting from the IDP implementation. Share success stories and demonstrate the positive outcomes to employees. Highlight how the new system has improved efficiency, accuracy, and other relevant metrics. This celebration reinforces the benefits of IDP and encourages further adoption and support.

11. Adjust the Implementation Approach: Be flexible in adjusting the implementation approach based on feedback and

changing circumstances. Continuously assess the progress and effectiveness of the implementation, identify areas for improvement, and adapt the approach as needed. Agile methodologies can help navigate challenges and facilitate a more iterative and responsive implementation process.

12. Leadership Support and Engagement: Secure support from organizational leadership and ensure their active engagement throughout the IDP implementation. Leaders should visibly champion the change, communicate the importance of IDP, and actively participate in training sessions or town hall meetings. Their support and involvement demonstrate the organization's commitment to the change and motivate employees to embrace it.

By addressing change resistance and proactively overcoming challenges, organizations can promote a positive and supportive environment during the IDP implementation process. This facilitates successful adoption, minimizes disruption, and enables employees to fully leverage the benefits of the new system.

Understanding Legal and Compliance Requirements

When implementing an Intelligent Document Processing (IDP) system, it is essential to have a thorough understanding of legal and compliance requirements. Adhering to relevant laws, regulations, and industry standards is crucial to ensure the privacy, security, and integrity of sensitive information. This section provides details on understanding legal and compliance requirements during IDP implementation.

1. Identify Applicable Laws and Regulations: Identify the laws and regulations that are relevant to your organization and industry. This may include data protection regulations (e.g., GDPR, CCPA), industry-specific compliance requirements (e.g., HIPAA for healthcare), or record retention regulations. Consult legal experts or compliance officers to ensure comprehensive coverage of the relevant legal framework.
2. Understand Data Privacy and Protection: Understand the specific data privacy and protection requirements applicable to your organization. Determine how personal or sensitive information is handled, stored, and processed within the IDP system. Ensure compliance with regulations regarding data access, consent, encryption, data transfer, and retention periods. Implement appropriate security measures to protect data from unauthorized access or breaches.
3. Evaluate Data Ownership and Control: Understand the ownership and control of data within the IDP system. Clarify whether the data remains under the organization's control or if it is shared with third-party service providers. Ensure compliance with applicable regulations regarding data ownership, consent, and data processing agreements when involving external vendors or cloud-based solutions.
4. Maintain Data Accuracy and Integrity: Maintain the accuracy and integrity of data processed through the IDP system. Implement appropriate controls, validation mechanisms, and quality checks to ensure that the extracted data is reliable and

consistent. Develop processes for handling data discrepancies, exceptions, or errors promptly to prevent inaccuracies or compliance issues.

5. Implement Audit Trails and Logging: Implement audit trails and logging mechanisms within the IDP system to track user activities, system changes, and data processing events. Maintain detailed records of document processing activities, including timestamps, user actions, and system responses. This supports compliance with audit requirements and facilitates traceability in case of investigations or compliance audits.
6. Document Retention and Destruction: Understand the document retention and destruction requirements relevant to your industry and jurisdiction. Implement processes and policies to ensure that documents are retained for the required duration and disposed of securely when no longer needed. Maintain a record of document retention schedules and destruction processes to demonstrate compliance with legal requirements.
7. Address Cross-Border Data Transfers: If your organization operates globally or transfers data across international borders, consider the legal requirements for cross-border data transfers. Ensure compliance with applicable regulations, such as EU-US Privacy Shield or Standard Contractual Clauses, when transferring data between different jurisdictions.
8. Consult Legal and Compliance Experts: Engage legal and compliance experts to provide guidance and support throughout the IDP implementation. Seek their advice on interpreting legal requirements, assessing compliance risks, and establishing appropriate safeguards. Regularly consult with these experts to stay updated on any changes in the legal landscape that may impact the IDP system.
9. Conduct Risk Assessments: Perform comprehensive risk assessments to identify potential legal and compliance risks associated with the IDP implementation. Assess the potential impact of these risks on the organization, stakeholders, and data subjects. Develop mitigation strategies and controls to minimize the identified risks and ensure adherence to legal requirements.

10. Stay Abreast of Regulatory Updates: Regularly monitor updates and changes in relevant laws, regulations, and industry standards. Stay informed about emerging legal requirements or new guidelines that may affect IDP implementation. Establish mechanisms to disseminate regulatory updates within the organization and proactively adjust IDP processes or controls to remain compliant.
11. Establish a Compliance Framework: Develop a comprehensive compliance framework that outlines policies, procedures, and controls related to IDP implementation. Document the compliance measures in place, including data protection policies, access controls, data sharing agreements, incident response plans, and training programs. Regularly review and update the compliance framework to ensure it aligns with evolving legal and regulatory requirements.

By understanding legal and compliance requirements, organizations can effectively navigate the complexities of IDP implementation while ensuring data privacy, security, and compliance with applicable laws. Compliance should be an ongoing consideration, and organizations should proactively adapt their IDP systems and processes as legal requirements evolve.

Implementing Document Retention and Destruction Policies

Implementing document retention and destruction policies is crucial for organizations to manage their information lifecycle effectively, comply with legal and regulatory requirements, and mitigate potential risks. This section provides details on implementing document retention and destruction policies as part of an Intelligent Document Processing (IDP) implementation.

1. Identify Applicable Requirements: Identify the legal and regulatory requirements that govern document retention and destruction in your industry and jurisdiction. Consult legal experts, compliance officers, or industry-specific guidelines to ensure comprehensive coverage of the relevant requirements. Consider factors such as document types, retention periods, and

any specific rules regarding the destruction of sensitive information.

2. Conduct a Document Inventory: Conduct a thorough inventory of your organization's documents to identify the types of documents and their associated metadata. Classify documents based on their content, purpose, and legal or regulatory requirements. This inventory will serve as a foundation for developing document retention and destruction policies tailored to your organization's needs.
3. Define Retention Periods: Define appropriate retention periods for different document types based on legal requirements, business needs, and industry best practices. Consider factors such as statutory limitations, contractual obligations, tax regulations, or industry-specific regulations. Retention periods may vary depending on the document's content, significance, or potential legal implications.
4. Establish Access Controls: Implement access controls to restrict access to documents during their retention period. Limit document access to authorized personnel or specific user roles to ensure compliance with privacy and security requirements. Use document management systems or IDP platforms to enforce access controls, track document access, and maintain an audit trail of document interactions.
5. Document Destruction Procedures: Develop documented procedures for the secure and systematic destruction of documents once their retention periods expire. Consider legal and regulatory requirements for the destruction process, including methods, verification, and documentation of destruction. Determine whether physical documents should be shredded, pulped, or securely disposed of, and ensure digital documents are permanently deleted.
6. Implement Data Redaction Techniques: Implement data redaction techniques to remove or mask sensitive information from documents before destruction. Redaction ensures that any confidential or personally identifiable information is appropriately protected during the retention and destruction

process. Use automated redaction tools or manual processes to redact sensitive information, ensuring compliance with privacy regulations.

7. Establish Document Destruction Protocols: Establish clear protocols for document destruction that outline responsibilities, methods, and timelines. Document destruction should involve authorized personnel, such as records managers or compliance officers, who are trained in handling sensitive information securely. Ensure that destruction protocols cover physical and digital documents, including backups, archives, or cloud-based storage.
8. Monitor and Document Destruction Activities: Maintain records of document destruction activities, including dates, methods used, and responsible parties. This documentation demonstrates compliance with legal and regulatory requirements and supports accountability and transparency. Regularly review and audit destruction activities to ensure adherence to established policies and identify any areas for improvement.
9. Train Employees: Provide comprehensive training to employees regarding document retention and destruction policies. Ensure they understand their responsibilities, the importance of compliance, and the consequences of non-compliance. Train employees on how to identify documents subject to retention or destruction policies and provide clear instructions on following the established protocols.

10. Regular Policy Review and Update: Regularly review and update document retention and destruction policies to align with evolving legal, regulatory, and business requirements. Periodically assess the effectiveness of existing policies and revise them, as necessary. Stay informed about changes in the legal landscape or industry best practices to ensure your policies remain up to date.

11. Document Retention and Destruction Governance: Establish governance mechanisms to oversee and monitor document retention and destruction practices within the organization. Assign responsibility to a designated individual or team for

policy enforcement, monitoring compliance, and addressing any non-compliance issues. Develop a process for reporting and addressing document retention and destruction-related incidents or breaches.

By implementing document retention and destruction policies, organizations can effectively manage their information lifecycle, reduce legal and compliance risks, and ensure the privacy and security of sensitive information. These policies should be documented, communicated to employees, and regularly reviewed and updated to maintain compliance with applicable laws and regulations.

Conducting Audits and Ensuring Compliance with Industry Standards

Conducting regular audits and ensuring compliance with industry standards are vital components of an effective Intelligent Document Processing (IDP) implementation. Audits help organizations assess their adherence to legal and regulatory requirements, identify gaps, and implement corrective actions. This section provides details on conducting audits and ensuring compliance with industry standards during the IDP implementation process.

1. Identify Relevant Standards and Regulations: Identify the industry-specific standards and regulations that apply to your organization. Examples may include ISO standards, industry-specific compliance frameworks, or data protection regulations such as GDPR or HIPAA. Stay updated on changes to these standards and regulations to ensure ongoing compliance.
2. Establish Compliance Framework: Develop a compliance framework that outlines the policies, procedures, and controls necessary to ensure adherence to relevant industry standards and regulations. The framework should include guidelines for document management, data protection, access controls, data retention, and other relevant aspects of IDP implementation. Clearly document the roles and responsibilities of individuals responsible for compliance.
3. Define Audit Scope and Objectives: Determine the scope and objectives of the audit process. Identify the areas, processes, or

systems that will be audited, such as document management practices, data security controls, access management, or compliance with specific regulations. Define clear objectives for the audit, such as assessing compliance, identifying risks, or evaluating the effectiveness of controls.

4. Develop Audit Procedures and Checklists: Develop detailed audit procedures and checklists to guide the audit process. These procedures should include step-by-step instructions on how to assess compliance with specific requirements or controls. The checklists can serve as a tool to systematically evaluate different aspects of the IDP implementation and identify any non-compliance or gaps.
5. Conduct Regular Internal Audits: Perform internal audits at regular intervals to assess compliance with industry standards and regulations. Internal audits can be conducted by dedicated internal audit teams or assigned to individuals with expertise in the relevant areas. Document the audit findings, including any non-compliance issues, and propose corrective actions to address identified gaps.
6. Engage External Auditors: Consider engaging external auditors to conduct independent audits of your IDP implementation. External auditors bring an objective perspective and specialized expertise to assess compliance and identify areas for improvement. Engage reputable audit firms or consultants with experience in the relevant industry standards and regulations.
7. Perform Compliance Gap Analysis: Conduct a compliance gap analysis to identify any deviations or gaps between your current practices and the requirements of industry standards and regulations. This analysis helps identify areas where additional controls, processes, or training may be necessary to ensure compliance. Develop and implement corrective actions to address identified gaps.
8. Remediate Non-Compliance Issues: If non-compliance issues are identified during the audit process, take prompt and appropriate actions to remediate them. Develop and implement corrective action plans to address non-compliance issues and

ensure that they are resolved effectively and in a timely manner. Document the remediation efforts and track their progress.

9. Maintain Documentation and Audit Trails: Maintain accurate and comprehensive documentation related to your IDP implementation and compliance efforts. Document policies, procedures, controls, audit findings, remediation actions, and any other relevant information. Maintain an audit trail that captures changes, access logs, and other critical information to facilitate transparency and accountability.
10. Continuous Monitoring and Improvement: Establish mechanisms for continuous monitoring and improvement of compliance efforts. Regularly review and update policies, procedures, and controls to reflect changes in industry standards and regulatory requirements. Monitor the effectiveness of controls, conduct periodic assessments, and refine compliance processes to ensure ongoing compliance.
11. Stay Updated with Regulatory Changes: Stay abreast of changes in industry standards and regulatory requirements that may impact your IDP implementation. Monitor updates from regulatory authorities, industry associations, or compliance forums to ensure that your organization remains compliant with the latest requirements. Proactively adapt your IDP processes and controls to address any new compliance obligations.

By conducting regular audits and ensuring compliance with industry standards and regulations, organizations can demonstrate their commitment to maintaining high standards of data protection, security, and regulatory compliance. The audit process helps identify areas for improvement and drives continuous improvement in the IDP implementation, ensuring a robust and compliant document management system.

CHAPTER 18: IDP FOR SPECIFIC INDUSTRIES AND USE CASES

Overview: Chapter 18 focuses on exploring the application of Intelligent Document Processing (IDP) in specific industries and use cases. While IDP has broad applicability across various sectors, this chapter delves into how IDP can be tailored to address the unique document management challenges and requirements of specific industries. It also highlights the use cases where IDP can deliver significant benefits and transformative outcomes. The chapter begins by introducing the concept of industry-specific IDP solutions and the importance of customizing IDP processes and technologies to align with industry-specific regulations, standards, and workflows. It emphasizes the need to understand the nuances and complexities of different industries to effectively implement IDP solutions.

The chapter then delves into specific industries and use cases where IDP can be leveraged effectively. It provides detailed insights, examples, and recommendations for implementing IDP in the following sectors:

1. Healthcare: Explore how IDP can streamline medical records management, automate insurance claims processing, improve patient data extraction, and ensure compliance with privacy regulations like HIPAA.
2. Financial Services: Examine the use of IDP in automating loan processing, invoice management, compliance document handling, anti-money laundering (AML) compliance, and Know Your Customer (KYC) processes.
3. Legal: Discover how IDP can enhance legal document management, automate contract review and analysis, streamline e-discovery processes, and improve legal research and case management.
4. Insurance: Learn about the application of IDP in automating policy administration, claims processing, underwriting, fraud detection, and regulatory compliance in the insurance industry.

5. Government: Explore how IDP can be leveraged to digitize government records, automate permit and licensing processes, optimize document-intensive workflows, and enhance citizen service delivery.
6. Manufacturing and Supply Chain: Understand how IDP can streamline invoice processing, purchase order management, quality control documentation, and compliance with industry regulations and standards in manufacturing and supply chain operations.
7. Human Resources: Discover the benefits of using IDP in automating employee onboarding, managing personnel records, processing resumes and job applications, and ensuring compliance with HR regulations.

Each industry-specific section provides insights into the challenges faced by the industry, the potential benefits of IDP implementation, and practical strategies for successful deployment. It includes case studies, best practices, and recommendations for tailoring IDP processes to meet industry-specific requirements.

The chapter concludes by emphasizing the importance of understanding the unique characteristics and needs of each industry and aligning the IDP implementation accordingly. It encourages organizations to explore the possibilities of IDP in their specific sectors and leverage its capabilities to achieve greater efficiency, accuracy, compliance, and customer satisfaction.

By delving into industry-specific applications and use cases, this chapter equips readers with the knowledge and guidance needed to implement IDP solutions effectively in their respective industries, unlocking the full potential of intelligent document processing for transformative outcomes.

IDP in Banking and Financial Services

The banking and financial services industry handles an extensive volume of documents and data, making it an ideal candidate for Intelligent Document Processing (IDP) solutions. IDP can help streamline document-intensive processes, enhance operational efficiency, improve compliance, and deliver better customer experiences. This section provides details on the application of IDP in banking and financial services.

1. Loan Processing: IDP can automate and expedite loan processing workflows, reducing manual effort and streamlining document verification and underwriting processes. IDP can extract relevant information from loan applications, financial statements, credit reports, and other supporting documents, ensuring accurate and efficient loan origination processes.
2. Invoice and Payment Processing: Automating invoice and payment processing using IDP can improve speed, accuracy, and efficiency. IDP solutions can extract invoice data, match it with purchase orders and contracts, perform validation checks, and facilitate seamless payment processing. This minimizes errors, reduces processing time, and enhances financial control and auditability.
3. Compliance Document Management: IDP plays a crucial role in managing compliance-related documents, such as regulatory filings, risk assessments, customer due diligence, and Anti-Money Laundering (AML) documentation. IDP can automate document classification, extract critical information for compliance checks, and facilitate audit trails to ensure regulatory compliance.
4. Know Your Customer (KYC) Processes: KYC processes involve extensive document verification and customer due diligence. IDP can automate the extraction of customer data from identification documents, proof of address, and other relevant documents. This streamlines KYC procedures, improves accuracy, and enhances the speed of customer onboarding.
5. Fraud Detection and Prevention: IDP can aid in fraud detection and prevention by automatically analyzing and cross-referencing various documents and data sources. It can identify suspicious activities, anomalies, and potential fraud patterns. IDP can flag high-risk transactions, verify customer

information, and enhance fraud prevention measures within the banking and financial services environment.

6. Compliance Reporting and Audit Support: IDP solutions assist in generating compliance reports and provide audit support by automating data extraction from financial statements, transaction records, and other relevant documents. This simplifies the process of producing accurate reports and ensures compliance with regulatory requirements.
7. Customer Correspondence and Support: IDP can improve customer service by automating the processing of customer inquiries, complaints, and service requests. By capturing and extracting information from customer correspondence, IDP enables efficient routing, response management, and analysis of customer interactions, leading to enhanced customer experiences.
8. Contract Management: IDP can simplify contract management processes by automating contract creation, extraction of key terms and conditions, and contract analysis. IDP solutions enable efficient contract lifecycle management, ensure compliance with contract obligations, and improve contract visibility and accessibility.
9. Investment and Wealth Management: IDP can streamline document-intensive processes within investment and wealth management, such as portfolio management, client reporting, trade confirmations, and compliance documentation. It facilitates efficient extraction of investment data, automates document classification, and enhances data-driven decision-making.

Implementing IDP in banking and financial services can drive significant benefits, including increased operational efficiency, reduced costs, improved compliance, enhanced risk management, and better customer experiences. By automating document-centric processes, organizations in this industry can focus on core activities, enhance accuracy, and stay competitive in a rapidly evolving landscape.

IDP in Healthcare and Medical Records Management

Healthcare organizations generate a massive amount of documentation, making effective document management critical for efficient operations and quality patient care. Intelligent Document Processing (IDP) solutions can significantly streamline medical records management, automate administrative tasks, and enhance compliance in the healthcare industry. This section provides details on the application of IDP in healthcare and medical records management.

1. Medical Records Digitization: IDP plays a crucial role in digitizing and organizing paper-based medical records. By scanning and extracting information from physical documents, IDP enables the conversion of paper records into searchable digital formats. This enhances accessibility, reduces storage costs, and improves information retrieval for healthcare professionals.
2. Electronic Health Record (EHR) Management: IDP solutions can automate the processing and management of electronic health records. IDP systems extract relevant data from EHRs, such as patient demographics, medical history, diagnoses, and treatment plans. This streamlines workflows, enables faster data access, and supports better decision-making for healthcare providers.
3. Document Classification and Organization: IDP facilitates the automatic classification and organization of various healthcare documents. It can categorize documents based on document types, such as lab reports, medical imaging, prescriptions, and consent forms. This simplifies document retrieval, improves accuracy, and enhances overall document management efficiency.
4. Patient Data Extraction: IDP solutions excel in extracting pertinent information from various patient-related documents. For instance, IDP can extract data from medical forms, insurance claims, laboratory results, and physician notes. This

automated extraction reduces manual effort, minimizes errors, and enables faster data analysis and decision-making.

5. Claims Processing and Billing: IDP automates the extraction of relevant data from insurance claims, medical invoices, and other billing documents. It accelerates claims processing, improves accuracy in billing coding, and reduces the risk of revenue leakage. By automating these administrative tasks, healthcare organizations can optimize their revenue cycle management.
6. Compliance with Privacy Regulations: IDP supports healthcare organizations in ensuring compliance with privacy regulations, such as the Health Insurance Portability and Accountability Act (HIPAA). IDP solutions can identify and redact sensitive patient information, such as social security numbers or personal health identifiers, from documents, ensuring patient data privacy and security.
7. Clinical Trial Document Management: IDP assists in managing the extensive documentation involved in clinical trials. It automates the extraction of data from clinical trial protocols, informed consent forms, adverse event reports, and other trial-related documents. This accelerates the review process, ensures regulatory compliance, and improves overall trial efficiency.
8. Streamlining Healthcare Workflows: IDP can automate various healthcare workflows, such as patient registration, appointment scheduling, referral management, and discharge processes. It eliminates manual data entry, reduces administrative burdens, and improves the efficiency of healthcare operations. This allows healthcare providers to focus more on patient care.
9. Data Analytics and Population Health Management: IDP solutions facilitate data analytics by extracting and standardizing data from healthcare documents. This enables better analysis of patient populations, disease patterns, treatment outcomes, and quality metrics. By harnessing this information, healthcare organizations can improve population health management initiatives and enhance patient care delivery.

Implementing IDP in healthcare and medical records management can enhance operational efficiency, improve patient care, and ensure regulatory compliance. By automating document-intensive processes, healthcare organizations can minimize manual errors, reduce administrative burdens, and allocate more time and resources to providing quality care to patients.

IDP in Legal and Contract Management

The legal industry deals with an extensive volume of documents, contracts, and legal correspondence, making Intelligent Document Processing (IDP) solutions invaluable for improving efficiency, accuracy, and compliance. IDP can significantly streamline legal document management, contract analysis, and various legal processes. This section provides details on the application of IDP in legal and contract management.

1. Legal Document Management: IDP facilitates the efficient management of legal documents, including contracts, pleadings, court filings, and legal correspondence. It automates the categorization, indexing, and retrieval of documents based on content and metadata, making it easier for legal professionals to locate and access information quickly.
2. Contract Analysis and Extraction: IDP can automate contract analysis by extracting critical information such as parties involved, key terms and conditions, dates, and obligations. This automated extraction enables faster contract review, analysis, and comparison, improving efficiency and accuracy in contract management.
3. E-Discovery: IDP plays a crucial role in e-discovery, which involves the identification, collection, and analysis of electronically stored information (ESI) for legal cases. IDP solutions can streamline the review process by automatically identifying and categorizing relevant documents, reducing manual effort and enabling more efficient e-discovery workflows.
4. Legal Research: IDP can enhance legal research by automating the extraction of relevant information from legal texts, court

opinions, and precedents. By automatically identifying and summarizing key legal concepts, IDP enables legal professionals to conduct research more efficiently and effectively.

5. Contract Lifecycle Management: IDP can automate various stages of the contract lifecycle, including contract creation, negotiation, execution, and renewal. It enables the extraction of data from contracts, such as key dates, parties, and obligations, and facilitates proactive contract management, compliance monitoring, and timely renewals.
6. Due Diligence: IDP solutions can streamline due diligence processes by automating the review and extraction of information from legal documents. This helps identify potential risks, discrepancies, or non-compliance issues in contracts, agreements, or legal filings, facilitating more efficient due diligence assessments.
7. Legal Case Management: IDP supports legal case management by automating the processing and organization of case-related documents, pleadings, and court filings. It enables the extraction of case information, relevant dates, and key events, making it easier for legal professionals to manage case documentation and deadlines effectively.
8. Compliance Documentation: IDP assists in managing compliance-related documents, such as regulatory filings, internal policies, and compliance reports. It automates the extraction of relevant data, verifies compliance with legal and regulatory requirements, and ensures accurate and timely submission of compliance documentation.
9. Redlining and Version Control: IDP solutions can automate the redlining process by identifying changes between different versions of contracts or legal documents. This streamlines the review process, facilitates collaboration, and ensures accurate tracking of document revisions.

Implementing IDP in legal and contract management processes can result in significant benefits, including increased productivity, improved accuracy, enhanced compliance, and reduced manual effort. By automating document-intensive tasks, legal professionals can focus more on strategic activities, provide better client service, and optimize overall legal operations.

Chapter 19: Future Trends in IDP

Overview: Chapter 19 explores the future trends and advancements in Intelligent Document Processing (IDP). As technology continues to evolve, IDP is expected to undergo significant transformations, offering new capabilities and opportunities for organizations. This chapter provides an overview of the emerging trends and potential developments in the field of IDP.

1. Artificial Intelligence (AI) Advancements: AI technologies, such as machine learning and natural language processing, will continue to advance, enabling IDP systems to become more intelligent and accurate. AI algorithms will be trained on vast amounts of data, leading to improved document understanding, classification, and data extraction capabilities.
2. Enhanced Natural Language Processing (NLP): NLP techniques will evolve to better understand and interpret complex documents and unstructured data. Advanced NLP models will be able to extract meaning, context, and relationships from documents, enabling more sophisticated analysis and decision-making.
3. Deep Learning and Neural Networks: Deep learning algorithms and neural networks will be employed to tackle complex IDP tasks, such as document classification, entity recognition, and data extraction. These techniques will enable more accurate and context-aware processing, improving the overall performance of IDP systems.
4. Hyperautomation and Intelligent Workflows: IDP will be integrated with other automation technologies, such as robotic process automation (RPA), to enable end-to-end process automation and intelligent workflows. Hyperautomation will leverage IDP's capabilities to automate document-related tasks within broader business processes.

5. Advanced Data Analytics: IDP systems will offer more advanced data analytics capabilities, enabling organizations to gain deeper insights from their document repositories. By analyzing extracted data, organizations can identify patterns, trends, and anomalies, leading to enhanced decision-making and improved operational efficiency.
6. Enhanced Security and Privacy Measures: With the increasing focus on data security and privacy, IDP systems will incorporate advanced encryption, access controls, and anonymization techniques. Data protection regulations and privacy concerns will drive the development of robust security measures within IDP solutions.
7. Cloud-Based IDP Solutions: Cloud-based IDP solutions will gain prominence, offering scalability, flexibility, and ease of implementation. Cloud platforms will enable organizations to leverage IDP capabilities without the need for extensive infrastructure investments, facilitating faster deployment and integration.
8. Integration with Emerging Technologies: IDP will integrate with emerging technologies such as blockchain, Internet of Things (IoT), and edge computing. These integrations will enable secure and seamless data sharing, improved traceability, and enhanced real-time document processing capabilities.
9. Augmented Collaboration and Human-in-the-Loop: IDP systems will increasingly focus on augmenting human intelligence and collaboration rather than replacing human involvement. Human-in-the-loop approaches will allow human reviewers to provide feedback, validate results, and continuously train and improve IDP models.
10. Industry-Specific IDP Solutions: IDP will continue to evolve with industry-specific solutions tailored to the unique needs of various sectors. These solutions will address specific regulatory requirements, document types, and workflows, providing organizations with more specialized and efficient IDP implementations.

By keeping abreast of these future trends and advancements, organizations can proactively adapt their IDP strategies, embrace emerging technologies, and leverage the full potential of IDP to optimize document management, improve operational efficiency, and drive innovation in their respective industries.

AI Advances and the Evolution of IDP

Artificial Intelligence (AI) advancements play a pivotal role in shaping the evolution of Intelligent Document Processing (IDP). As AI technologies continue to progress, IDP systems are becoming more sophisticated, intelligent, and capable of processing and understanding complex documents. This section explores the AI advances driving the evolution of IDP.

1. Machine Learning (ML) Algorithms: ML algorithms are at the heart of IDP systems. As AI techniques advance, ML models used in IDP are becoming more powerful and accurate. Algorithms such as convolutional neural networks (CNNs) and recurrent neural networks (RNNs) are employed for tasks like document classification, entity recognition, and data extraction. ML algorithms are trained on large datasets, enabling IDP systems to continuously learn and improve over time.
2. Natural Language Processing (NLP): NLP plays a crucial role in IDP, particularly for understanding and extracting information from unstructured text in documents. With AI advancements, NLP techniques are becoming more sophisticated, allowing IDP systems to comprehend the context, semantics, and relationships within documents. Advanced NLP models can accurately extract key data points, understand complex language structures, and improve overall document comprehension.
3. Deep Learning and Neural Networks: Deep learning techniques, powered by neural networks, have revolutionized IDP. Deep learning models can automatically learn hierarchical representations of documents, enabling more accurate and robust document analysis. Deep learning architectures, such as

transformers, have significantly improved IDP capabilities, enabling tasks like document summarization, sentiment analysis, and named entity recognition.

4. Transfer Learning and Pretrained Models: Transfer learning, a technique where models trained on one task are repurposed for another, is advancing IDP capabilities. Pretrained models, such as BERT (Bidirectional Encoder Representations from Transformers), can be fine-tuned for specific IDP tasks. This approach allows IDP systems to leverage the knowledge acquired from vast amounts of data and pretrained models, resulting in better performance even with limited training data.
5. Explainability and Interpretability: With the evolution of AI in IDP, there is a growing focus on explainability and interpretability. AI models are becoming more transparent, allowing users to understand the reasoning behind their decisions. Techniques like attention mechanisms and model interpretability methods enable IDP systems to provide explanations for document classifications, data extractions, and decision-making processes.
6. Reinforcement Learning (RL) Integration: While still in its early stages in IDP, reinforcement learning has the potential to enhance IDP capabilities further. RL techniques can be used to optimize IDP workflows, automate decision-making processes, and improve the overall efficiency of IDP systems. By training AI agents through trial and error, reinforcement learning can enable IDP systems to adapt and learn from feedback.
7. Continuous Learning and Adaptive Systems: AI advances are driving the development of IDP systems that can continuously learn and adapt. Instead of static models, IDP systems can be designed to incorporate feedback loops, enabling continuous improvement based on user interactions and evolving document patterns. These adaptive systems can adapt to new document formats, languages, and evolving requirements without the need for extensive retraining.
8. Human-in-the-Loop Approaches: The evolution of IDP emphasizes the importance of human expertise and

collaboration. Human-in-the-loop approaches allow human reviewers to provide feedback, validate results, and continuously train and refine IDP models. By combining the strengths of AI and human intelligence, these approaches enhance the accuracy and reliability of IDP systems.

As AI advances continue to shape the field, IDP systems are becoming more accurate, efficient, and adaptable. The integration of AI techniques, such as machine learning, natural language processing, and deep learning, enables IDP to handle complex document processing tasks with increased accuracy and automation. The evolving AI landscape promises further advancements in IDP, driving the transformation of document management and revolutionizing the way organizations handle information.

Intelligent Automation and Robotic Process Automation (RPA)

Intelligent Automation (IA) and Robotic Process Automation (RPA) are two powerful technologies that are revolutionizing business processes across various industries. While they have distinct characteristics, their combination can deliver significant benefits by automating repetitive tasks, improving efficiency, and enhancing overall productivity. This section explores the details of Intelligent Automation and Robotic Process Automation.

1. Robotic Process Automation (RPA): RPA refers to the use of software robots or "bots" to automate repetitive, rule-based tasks traditionally performed by humans. RPA bots can mimic human interactions with digital systems, such as navigating applications, entering data, extracting information, and performing predefined actions. RPA is highly effective in automating routine tasks that involve structured data and follow clear rules and instructions.
2. Intelligent Automation (IA): Intelligent Automation goes beyond RPA by incorporating Artificial Intelligence (AI) technologies, such as machine learning, natural language processing, and cognitive capabilities. IA systems can learn, adapt, and make intelligent decisions based on data analysis and

pattern recognition. IA leverages AI to automate complex tasks that involve unstructured data, require decision-making, and exhibit a level of cognitive understanding.

3. Benefits of RPA: RPA offers several benefits to organizations, including increased efficiency, accuracy, and scalability. By automating repetitive tasks, RPA eliminates human errors, reduces processing time, and allows employees to focus on more strategic and value-added activities. RPA also offers scalability as bots can handle multiple processes simultaneously, accommodating fluctuations in workload without the need for additional resources.
4. Benefits of IA: IA brings additional benefits by combining AI technologies with automation. It enables the automation of complex tasks that involve unstructured data, such as document processing, natural language understanding, and sentiment analysis. IA systems can learn from data, make predictions, and continuously improve their performance over time. This results in enhanced decision-making capabilities, improved customer experiences, and the ability to handle more sophisticated business processes.
5. Combined Impact: The combination of RPA and IA creates a powerful automation ecosystem. RPA provides the foundation for automating structured and rule-based tasks, while IA adds cognitive capabilities to handle unstructured data and perform more advanced tasks. Together, they enable end-to-end process automation, integrating various systems and applications, and orchestrating complex workflows across departments and functions.
6. Use Cases: RPA and IA find application in a wide range of industries and business functions. Common use cases include data entry and data migration, invoice processing, customer onboarding, claims processing, HR administration, and IT support. IA can be particularly valuable in tasks that involve document processing, natural language understanding, sentiment analysis, and decision-making based on unstructured data.

7. Considerations for Implementation: When implementing RPA and IA, organizations should consider factors such as process suitability, technology compatibility, security, governance, and change management. Identifying the right processes for automation, ensuring compatibility with existing systems, addressing security and compliance requirements, establishing governance frameworks, and effectively managing the human-machine collaboration are crucial for successful implementation.
8. Future Trends: The future of IA and RPA involves advancements in AI technologies, such as machine learning, natural language understanding, and computer vision. Continued integration with IDP, cloud computing, and emerging technologies like blockchain and IoT will further expand the capabilities of IA and RPA. The focus will be on intelligent automation, where AI-enabled bots can handle end-to-end processes, make informed decisions, and continuously learn and adapt.

Intelligent Automation and Robotic Process Automation are transformative technologies that enable organizations to automate and optimize their processes, enhance efficiency, and improve overall business outcomes. By leveraging the strengths of both technologies, organizations can achieve higher levels of automation and unlock new possibilities for innovation and growth.

Integration with Emerging Technologies (e.g., Blockchain, IoT)

Intelligent Document Processing (IDP) systems can be enhanced by integrating them with emerging technologies, such as blockchain and the Internet of Things (IoT). These technologies provide unique capabilities that can further optimize document management processes, enhance security, and enable new possibilities for data exchange and collaboration. This section explores the details of integrating IDP with blockchain and IoT.

1. Integration with Blockchain: Blockchain is a decentralized, distributed ledger technology that offers immutability, transparency, and security. By integrating IDP with blockchain, several benefits can be realized:

a. Document Integrity and Traceability: IDP systems can leverage blockchain to create a tamper-proof and auditable record of document transactions. Each document update or access can be recorded on the blockchain, ensuring document integrity and providing a transparent audit trail.

b. Authentication and Verification: Blockchain-based identity management systems can be integrated with IDP to verify the authenticity of users and documents. This helps establish trust and ensures that only authorized individuals can access and modify sensitive documents.

c. Smart Contracts: IDP can be combined with blockchain-based smart contracts to automate document-related processes. Smart contracts can automatically trigger actions or conditions based on predefined rules, streamlining tasks such as document signing, approval workflows, and payment processing.

d. Supply Chain Management: Integrating IDP with blockchain can enhance supply chain visibility and traceability. Documents such as invoices, shipping records, and quality certificates can be stored on the blockchain, enabling secure sharing and verification across the supply chain.

2. Integration with the Internet of Things (IoT): IoT involves connecting physical devices and sensors to the internet, enabling data collection and communication between devices. When integrated with IDP, IoT can offer several benefits:

a. Data Capture and Contextual Information: IoT devices can capture data from physical objects or environments and provide contextual information about documents. For example, sensors embedded in machines can automatically capture data about usage, maintenance, or performance, which can be linked to relevant documents for analysis and decision-making.

b. Real-time Data Integration: IDP systems can leverage real-time data from IoT devices to enhance document processing. For example, real-time sensor data can trigger document workflows, such as initiating maintenance requests or generating reports based on specific thresholds or events.

c. Enhanced Security and Access Control: IoT devices can be used to enforce physical and logical access controls for document management systems. For instance, access to sensitive documents can be granted based on the proximity of authorized individuals or the authentication of IoT devices.

d. Automation and Efficiency: IoT devices can automate data capture and document generation processes. For example, IoT-enabled devices in a manufacturing environment can automatically generate production reports or quality assurance documents based on real-time data feeds.

3. Combined Benefits: Integrating IDP with emerging technologies like blockchain and IoT offers combined benefits that go beyond individual capabilities. For example:

a. Enhanced Security and Privacy: The immutability and transparency of blockchain combined with IoT-based access controls can ensure secure document management and privacy.

b. Streamlined Processes: Blockchain-enabled smart contracts combined with IoT data can automate and streamline document-related processes, reducing manual effort and improving efficiency.

c. Improved Traceability: The integration of blockchain and IoT enables end-to-end traceability of documents, from creation to storage, access, and eventual disposal, providing a comprehensive audit trail.

d. Enhanced Collaboration: Blockchain-based decentralized document storage and IoT-enabled data sharing can facilitate secure and efficient collaboration among multiple stakeholders, ensuring data integrity and eliminating the need for intermediaries.

The integration of IDP with emerging technologies like blockchain and IoT opens up new possibilities for secure, efficient, and transparent document management. Organizations can leverage these technologies to enhance data integrity, streamline processes, improve collaboration, and unlock new opportunities for innovation and business growth.

CHAPTER 20: CASE STUDIES AND SUCCESS STORIES

Overview: Chapter 20 provides a collection of case studies and success stories that highlight the real-world implementation of Intelligent Document Processing (IDP) solutions. These case studies demonstrate how organizations from various industries have successfully leveraged IDP to improve their document management processes, increase efficiency, and achieve significant business outcomes. The chapter showcases the diverse applications and benefits of IDP through practical examples.

1. Industry-Specific Implementations: The case studies cover a range of industries, including banking and finance, healthcare, legal, manufacturing, and more. Each case study delves into the specific challenges faced by organizations within their respective industries and showcases how IDP solutions were tailored to address those challenges.
2. Document Management Optimization: The case studies highlight how IDP has transformed document management processes. They showcase the automation of document classification, data extraction, and validation, leading to reduced manual effort, improved accuracy, and faster processing times. Organizations have achieved streamlined workflows, enhanced compliance, and improved document accessibility and retrieval.
3. Improved Operational Efficiency: The case studies demonstrate how IDP has significantly improved operational efficiency for organizations. By automating document-centric tasks, organizations have experienced reduced processing time, eliminated errors, and optimized resource allocation. The case studies present metrics and quantifiable results that highlight the time and cost savings achieved through IDP implementation.
4. Enhanced Compliance and Risk Management: Several case studies focus on how IDP has helped organizations achieve better compliance and risk management. By automating

document review and ensuring accurate data extraction, organizations have improved compliance with regulatory requirements and reduced the risk of errors or non-compliance. The case studies highlight the impact of IDP on regulatory reporting, legal compliance, and audit processes.

5. Improved Customer Experience: Certain case studies showcase how IDP has positively impacted customer experiences. By streamlining document-intensive processes, organizations have achieved faster response times, improved accuracy in customer interactions, and enhanced document visibility for customers. The case studies highlight how IDP has improved customer onboarding, claims processing, and overall satisfaction.
6. Scalability and Flexibility: The case studies emphasize how IDP solutions have offered scalability and flexibility to organizations. They showcase how IDP has accommodated growing document volumes, integrated with existing systems, and adapted to evolving business needs. The case studies illustrate how organizations have scaled their IDP implementations to meet the demands of their operations.
7. ROI and Business Impact: The case studies provide insights into the return on investment (ROI) and business impact achieved through IDP implementation. They highlight cost savings, efficiency gains, and improved productivity resulting from streamlined document processes. The case studies demonstrate the tangible and measurable benefits organizations have realized by implementing IDP solutions.

By presenting real-world examples, the case studies and success stories in this chapter inspire and educate readers about the transformative power of IDP. They offer practical insights into the challenges faced, the solutions implemented, and the outcomes achieved by organizations across different industries. Readers can gain valuable knowledge, learn from best practices, and find inspiration for their own IDP journeys.

Real-World Examples of Successful IDP Implementations

1. Banking and Finance: A leading bank implemented an IDP solution to automate the processing of loan applications. The system automatically extracted relevant data from customer documents, such as income statements and identification documents, and validated the information for accuracy. This significantly reduced the manual effort required for application processing, improved turnaround time, and enhanced compliance with regulatory requirements.
2. Healthcare: A large hospital implemented an IDP solution to streamline medical record management. The system automatically digitized and categorized patient records, extracting key information such as medical history, diagnoses, and treatment plans. This enabled healthcare professionals to access patient information quickly, resulting in improved care coordination, reduced errors, and enhanced patient outcomes.
3. Legal Services: A law firm integrated IDP into their document management processes to streamline contract analysis and review. The system automated the extraction of key contract terms, dates, and obligations, allowing legal professionals to quickly review and compare contract terms. This led to faster contract turnaround times, reduced risk, and improved client satisfaction.
4. Manufacturing: A manufacturing company implemented IDP to automate invoice processing. The system automatically extracted invoice data, validated it against purchase orders and delivery receipts, and initiated payment workflows. This eliminated manual data entry, reduced invoice processing time, minimized errors, and improved cash flow management.
5. Insurance: An insurance company utilized IDP to automate claims processing. The system extracted relevant data from claim forms, policy documents, and supporting evidence, enabling faster claims assessment and decision-making. This resulted in reduced claims processing time, improved accuracy in claims assessment, and enhanced customer satisfaction.
6. Government: A government agency implemented IDP to streamline document management for permit applications. The

system automated the extraction of applicant information, verification of supporting documents, and generation of permits. This improved processing efficiency, reduced administrative burden, and enhanced transparency in the permit application process.

7. Human Resources: A multinational company deployed IDP to automate employee onboarding processes. The system automatically extracted employee data from application forms, verified identification documents, and generated employee records. This streamlined the onboarding process, reduced manual errors, and improved data accuracy in HR systems.
8. Retail: A retail chain implemented IDP to automate invoice reconciliation processes. The system automatically matched invoices with purchase orders and delivery receipts, validated prices and quantities, and flagged discrepancies for review. This accelerated the invoice reconciliation process, minimized errors, and improved financial accuracy and reporting.

These real-world examples highlight the diverse applications of IDP across industries and demonstrate the tangible benefits organizations have achieved through successful implementations. By automating document-intensive processes, organizations have improved efficiency, reduced errors, enhanced compliance, and ultimately transformed their operations for better business outcomes.

Lessons Learned and Best Practices from Industry Leaders

Industry leaders who have successfully implemented Intelligent Document Processing (IDP) have gained valuable insights and identified best practices that can guide organizations embarking on their IDP journey. Here are some key lessons learned and best practices from industry leaders:

1. Start with a Clear Strategy: Define clear objectives and align the IDP implementation with your organization's strategic goals. Identify the specific pain points, document management challenges, and desired outcomes that you aim to achieve through IDP.

2. Conduct a Thorough Assessment: Before implementing IDP, assess your document management needs, including document types, volumes, and complexities. Analyze existing processes, identify bottlenecks, and determine areas where IDP can provide the most value. This assessment will help you tailor the implementation to your specific requirements.
3. Engage Stakeholders: Involve key stakeholders from different departments, including IT, operations, legal, and compliance, in the IDP implementation process. Their insights and perspectives will ensure that the solution aligns with organizational needs and secures necessary support and buy-in.
4. Prioritize Data Quality: Data quality is crucial for successful IDP implementation. Invest time and effort in ensuring the accuracy and consistency of your data. Clean and standardized data will lead to more accurate document processing and better outcomes.
5. Choose the Right IDP Solution: Select an IDP solution that aligns with your organization's requirements, scalability, and integration capabilities. Consider factors such as accuracy, scalability, flexibility, ease of use, vendor support, and compliance with industry regulations.
6. Pilot and Iterate: Start with a pilot implementation of IDP in a specific department or process. Test and validate the solution, gather feedback, and make necessary adjustments before scaling up the implementation. Iterative implementation allows you to fine-tune the solution based on real-world experiences.
7. Invest in Training and Change Management: Provide comprehensive training to users and stakeholders involved in the IDP implementation. Ensure that they understand the benefits, functionalities, and proper utilization of the IDP solution. Address change management challenges by communicating the value proposition of IDP and engaging employees in the transition.
8. Focus on Integration: Integrate IDP with existing systems, such as content management systems, customer relationship management (CRM) platforms, or enterprise resource planning

(ERP) systems. Seamless integration allows for smooth data flow, reduces duplication, and enhances overall process efficiency.

9. Monitor Performance and Continuously Improve: Establish key performance indicators (KPIs) to measure the effectiveness of IDP. Monitor performance metrics, identify areas for improvement, and make adjustments as needed. Continuous improvement and optimization are essential for maximizing the benefits of IDP.
10. Stay Updated on Industry Trends: Keep abreast of the latest trends, advancements, and best practices in IDP. Attend industry conferences, participate in forums, and engage with industry experts to gain insights into emerging technologies, new techniques, and success stories from other organizations.

By incorporating these lessons learned and best practices, organizations can enhance their IDP implementations and maximize the benefits of document management automation. The experiences and expertise of industry leaders provide valuable guidance for organizations embarking on their IDP journey.

Inspiring Stories of Improved Efficiency and Cost Savings

Implementing Intelligent Document Processing (IDP) has resulted in significant efficiency gains and cost savings for many organizations. Here are some inspiring stories that showcase how IDP has transformed document management processes and generated tangible benefits:

1. Streamlined Accounts Payable Process: A large manufacturing company implemented IDP to automate their accounts payable process. By automatically capturing invoice data, validating information, and matching invoices with purchase orders, the company streamlined their invoice processing workflows. As a result, they achieved a 70% reduction in processing time, eliminated manual data entry errors, and significantly improved the accuracy of financial reporting. The automation also enabled

the finance team to handle a larger volume of invoices without hiring additional staff, resulting in substantial cost savings.

2. Accelerated Customer Onboarding: A leading financial institution incorporated IDP into their customer onboarding process. The system automated the extraction and validation of customer data from various documents, such as identification proofs and address verifications. By automating these tasks, the institution achieved a 50% reduction in onboarding time, improved data accuracy, and enhanced customer satisfaction. The streamlined process allowed the institution to onboard more customers with the same resources, resulting in increased revenue and reduced operational costs.
3. Improved Claims Processing in Insurance: An insurance company integrated IDP into their claims processing workflows. The system automatically extracted relevant data from claim forms, policy documents, and supporting evidence, eliminating the need for manual data entry. This led to a significant reduction in claims processing time, improved accuracy in claims assessment, and enhanced customer experiences. The company achieved a 40% reduction in claims processing costs, reduced error rates, and accelerated claims settlements, resulting in improved customer satisfaction and increased operational efficiency.
4. Enhanced Compliance and Audit Processes: A multinational corporation deployed IDP to automate their compliance and audit documentation processes. By automating the extraction of key information from compliance documents, the company improved the accuracy and efficiency of compliance assessments. The system also facilitated faster and more comprehensive audits by automating the retrieval of audit-related documents. As a result, the company achieved faster compliance reporting, reduced manual effort, and improved compliance outcomes, leading to potential cost savings in regulatory fines and penalties.
5. Efficient Contract Management: A legal firm implemented IDP to streamline their contract management processes. By

automating contract analysis, extraction of key terms, and comparison of contract clauses, the firm significantly reduced the time and effort required for contract reviews. This resulted in improved turnaround times, enhanced accuracy, and better risk management. The firm also achieved cost savings by reducing the need for external legal resources and optimizing their internal resources for higher-value activities.

6. Accelerated Mortgage Processing: A mortgage lender integrated IDP into their mortgage processing workflows. By automating the extraction and validation of customer data, income statements, and property documents, the lender achieved faster mortgage processing times and reduced manual errors. This streamlined process enabled the lender to handle a higher volume of mortgage applications, resulting in increased revenue and reduced processing costs. Additionally, the automation improved data accuracy and reduced the risk of compliance violations.

These inspiring stories demonstrate the transformative impact of IDP on efficiency gains and cost savings across various industries. By automating document-intensive processes, organizations have achieved significant improvements in productivity, accuracy, and customer experiences while optimizing resource allocation and reducing operational costs. These success stories serve as motivation for organizations seeking to harness the power of IDP to drive their own efficiency and cost-saving initiatives.

CHAPTER 21: APPENDIX - GLOSSARY OF IDP TERMS AND DEFINITIONS

To provide a comprehensive understanding of Intelligent Document Processing (IDP) and its associated terminology, this glossary offers definitions of key terms commonly used in the field. Whether you are new to IDP or seeking clarification on specific concepts, this glossary will serve as a valuable reference.

1. Intelligent Document Processing (IDP): The use of artificial intelligence (AI) and automation technologies to extract and process data from unstructured documents, such as invoices, contracts, and forms.
2. Document Management: The process of organizing, storing, and managing documents throughout their lifecycle, including creation, storage, retrieval, sharing, and disposal.
3. Data Extraction: The process of automatically identifying and capturing relevant data from documents, typically using techniques like optical character recognition (OCR) and natural language processing (NLP).
4. Optical Character Recognition (OCR): Technology that converts scanned images or printed text into machine-readable text using pattern recognition algorithms.
5. Natural Language Processing (NLP): The AI discipline concerned with the interaction between computers and human language, enabling computers to understand, interpret, and generate human language.
6. Machine Learning (ML): A subset of AI that enables computers to learn from data and improve performance on specific tasks without explicit programming.
7. Deep Learning: A subset of ML that uses artificial neural networks with multiple layers to learn hierarchical

representations of data, enabling more advanced analysis and understanding.

8. Neural Network: A computing system inspired by the structure and functioning of the human brain, consisting of interconnected artificial neurons that process and transmit information.
9. Unstructured Data: Data that does not have a predefined data model or organization, such as text documents, images, videos, and audio recordings.
10. Structured Data: Data that has a predefined data model or organization, typically organized in rows and columns in a database or spreadsheet.
11. Data Validation: The process of ensuring the accuracy, completeness, and consistency of extracted data through various checks and validations.
12. Classification: The process of categorizing documents based on their content, purpose, or characteristics, often using machine learning algorithms to automate the classification task.
13. Indexing: The process of assigning keywords or metadata to documents to facilitate their retrieval and organization.
14. Workflow Automation: The automation of sequential tasks and processes involved in document management, enabling efficient and streamlined document processing.
15. Business Process Automation: The use of technology to automate and streamline business processes, including document-intensive processes, to improve efficiency and productivity.
16. Accuracy: The degree to which IDP systems correctly extract and process data from documents without errors or inaccuracies.
17. Scalability: The ability of an IDP system to handle increasing volumes of documents and data processing without significant performance degradation.
18. Integration: The process of connecting IDP systems with other software applications, databases, or systems to enable seamless data exchange and process automation.

19. Data Security: The protection of sensitive data against unauthorized access, use, disclosure, modification, or destruction.
20. Compliance: The adherence to legal, regulatory, and industry-specific requirements and standards governing the processing and management of documents and data.
21. Audit Trail: A record of activities, transactions, or changes made to documents, providing a chronological history and ensuring transparency and accountability.
22. User Interface (UI): The graphical interface through which users interact with the IDP system, including features like document upload, data validation, and system configuration.
23. User Experience (UX): The overall experience and satisfaction of users when interacting with the IDP system, focusing on usability, efficiency, and effectiveness.
24. Return on Investment (ROI): The measure of the profitability or cost-effectiveness of an IDP implementation, comparing the benefits gained against the investment made.
25. Artificial Intelligence (AI): The simulation of human intelligence in machines that can perform tasks that typically require human intelligence, such as visual perception, speech recognition, and decision-making.
26. Robotic Process Automation (RPA): The use of software robots or "bots" to automate repetitive, rule-based tasks traditionally performed by humans.
27. Internet of Things (IoT): The network of physical devices, vehicles, appliances, and other objects embedded with sensors, software, and connectivity to exchange data and enable remote monitoring and control.
28. Blockchain: A decentralized and distributed digital ledger technology that securely records and verifies transactions across multiple computers or nodes.
29. Smart Contract: Self-executing contracts with predefined rules and conditions encoded on a blockchain, automatically triggering actions or events based on specific criteria.

30. Compliance Regulations: Legal and industry-specific regulations and standards that organizations must adhere to when processing and managing documents, such as General Data Protection Regulation (GDPR), Sarbanes-Oxley Act (SOX), and Health Insurance Portability and Accountability Act (HIPAA).

This glossary provides a foundation for understanding key IDP terms and concepts. As the field of IDP continues to evolve, it is essential to stay updated with the latest terminology and advancements. By familiarizing yourself with these definitions, you will be better equipped to navigate discussions, research, and implementation of IDP solutions.

Remember to adapt the chapters, tips, recommendations, and strategies to fit your specific needs and goals as you embark on your intelligent document processing journey. While the guide provides a comprehensive overview and best practices, it is crucial to tailor them to your organization's unique requirements and circumstances. Consider the following points as you customize your IDP implementation:

1. Assess Your Requirements: Conduct a thorough assessment of your document management needs, including the types of documents, volumes, complexities, and specific challenges you face. This will help you prioritize the areas where IDP can provide the most significant impact.
2. Define Clear Goals and Objectives: Set clear goals and objectives for your IDP implementation. Identify the specific outcomes you want to achieve, such as improved efficiency, cost savings, compliance, or enhanced customer experiences. Align these goals with your organization's strategic objectives.
3. Engage Stakeholders: Involve key stakeholders from different departments, such as IT, operations, legal, and compliance, throughout the IDP journey. Their insights and perspectives will ensure that the solution aligns with organizational needs and receives the necessary support and buy-in.

4. Continuously Monitor and Improve: Establish performance metrics and regularly monitor the effectiveness of your IDP implementation. Continuously evaluate the impact of IDP on your processes, track key performance indicators, and identify areas for improvement. Implement feedback loops and make necessary adjustments to optimize your IDP solution.
5. Prioritize Data Security and Compliance: Ensure that your IDP implementation adheres to data security and compliance regulations relevant to your industry. Implement appropriate access controls, encryption mechanisms, and data protection measures. Regularly review and update your security protocols to stay aligned with evolving regulations.
6. Foster Change Management and User Adoption: Recognize that implementing IDP involves a significant change in processes and workflows. Invest in change management efforts to communicate the benefits of IDP, address user concerns, and provide comprehensive training and support to ensure successful user adoption.
7. Stay Informed about Industry Trends: Keep yourself updated with the latest developments, emerging technologies, and best practices in IDP. Attend industry conferences, participate in forums, and engage with experts to stay ahead of the curve and leverage the potential of new advancements.

Remember, your IDP journey is unique to your organization, and customization is essential for success. Adapt the chapters, tips, recommendations, and strategies outlined in the guide to align with your specific needs, resources, and goals. Regularly evaluate and iterate on your implementation to ensure continuous improvement and maximum value from your IDP efforts. Good luck on your intelligent document processing journey!

CHAPTER 22: D & C

Disclaimer & Copyright

DISCLAIMER: The author and publisher have used their best efforts in preparing the information found in this book. The author and publisher make no representation or warranties with respect to the accuracy, applicability, fitness, or completeness of the contents of this book. The information contained in this book is strictly for educational purposes. Therefore, if you wish to apply ideas contained in this book, you are taking full responsibility for your actions. EVERY EFFORT HAS BEEN MADE TO ACCURATELY REPRESENT THIS PRODUCT AND IT'S POTENTIAL. HOWEVER, THERE IS NO GUARANTEE THAT YOU WILL IMPROVE IN ANY WAY USING THE TECHNIQUES AND IDEAS IN THESE MATERIALS. EXAMPLES IN THESE MATERIALS ARE NOT TO BE INTERPRETED AS A PROMISE OR GUARANTEE OF ANYTHING. IMPROVEMENT POTENTIAL IS ENTIRELY DEPENDENT ON THE PERSON USING THIS PRODUCTS, IDEAS AND TECHNIQUES. YOUR LEVEL OF IMPROVEMENT IN ATTAINING THE RESULTS CLAIMED IN OUR MATERIALS DEPENDS ON THE TIME YOU DEVOTE TO THE PROGRAM, IDEAS AND TECHNIQUES MENTIONED, KNOWLEDGE AND VARIOUS SKILLS. SINCE THESE FACTORS DIFFER ACCORDING TO INDIVIDUALS, WE CANNOT GUARANTEE YOUR SUCCESS OR IMPROVEMENT LEVEL. NOR ARE WE RESPONSIBLE FOR ANY OF YOUR ACTIONS. MANY FACTORS WILL BE IMPORTANT IN DETERMINING YOUR ACTUAL RESULTS AND NO GUARANTEES ARE MADE THAT YOU WILL ACHIEVE THE RESULTS. The author and publisher disclaim any warranties (express or implied), merchantability, or fitness for any particular purpose. The author and publisher shall in no event be held liable to any party for any direct, indirect, punitive, special, incidental or other consequential damages arising directly or indirectly from any use of this material, which is provided “as is”, and without warranties. As always, the advice of a competent professional should be sought. The author and publisher do not warrant the performance, effectiveness or applicability of any sites listed or linked to in this report. All links are for information purposes only and are not warranted for content, accuracy or any other implied or explicit purpose.

 First Printing, 2023

www.ingramcontent.com/pod-product-compliance
Lightning Source LLC
Chambersburg PA
CBHW060113120726
48003CB00009B/2613
* 9 7 9 8 2 2 3 4 1 7 3 0 9 *